MW00476079

All Is Calm

A Daily Reader From Thanksgiving to Christmas

Revised and Updated Edition 2021

By Randy Schlichting and Amy Shirley

All Is Calm: A Daily Reader from Thanksgiving to Christmas
Revised and Updated Edition
© 2021 Schlichting and Shirley Writings

ISBN 978-1-68564-036-1

The Gift Before the Gift

The holiday season is upon us. This little book is designed to help you walk into the season with perhaps a new sense of what the Lord is saying in and through, not just the holiday; but life.

We know you don't have a lot of time, so each day's reading will take about five minutes. You can leave it at that. Read and be on your way.

Or you can take the thought with you as you go about your business. You might find that the Lord uses it on the road. You might come back to it in the evening and dig a bit deeper using scripture as your guide. Or use the journaling space. Maybe you will talk about it with a friend. There are no rules here. This book is meant to be a gift before the gifts. It is for you, and we are hoping that it is from Him in some sense, just because He loves you.

Enjoy

Randy and Amy

About the Authors

Randy Schlichting

Randy has been blessed to participate in kingdom building at Perimeter Church for over 24 years under the leadership of Randy Pope and now Jeff Norris. He has developed and led various ministries, including discipleship and worship. Currently, he serves as the Pastor of Shepherding at Perimeter Church and the President and Dean of Administration and Development at Metro Atlanta Seminary.

He has been joyfully married to Dorothy for forty years. They love to minister together, and they love the beach. Together they have three daughters, three wonderful sons-in-law, and five grandchildren.

Amy Shirley

Amy is a life-long member of Perimeter Church which is where the collaboration for this book began. She is the Managing Partner and a Financial Advisor at Moore & Shirley Financial Planning, LLC.

She has been married to her college sweetheart, Josh, for more than 17 years. They enjoy serving together at the church and cheering on their college football team. Together, they have a son and daughter through the gift of adoption.

Looking Back

Nine years ago, Randy and I set out to write this little devotional book. At the time, my husband and I had been praying for the child or children that the Lord might have for us. We had been waiting for five years and had two and a half more years of waiting to go, though, of course, we did not know that at the time. As I write this, we now have two beautiful children through the gift of adoption. The holidays are lively and sweet these days. In the last year, my husband had an incredibly tough battle with cancer, and while the cancer appears to be gone, the recovery is slow and long.

In the past nine years, so much has changed, and yet the most important things remain the same. Now, more than ever, I have seen the need to slow down, seek to hear the Lord through His Word, and tune my heart to Him. I hope that this devotional is an encouragement and blessing to you as we walk into this holiday season.
  -Amy

Time flies! Amy still looks like she is the same age she was when we started. As for me, I have a few more wrinkles and a few less hairs on my head. During these years, I have seen a lot of pain, and I have experienced much joy with the sheep of His pasture. I am learning to see more clearly by slowing down.

I so agree with Amy that "slowing down" is needed for the soul to breathe and see. Walking through life at "three miles an hour" is about the speed the Lord walks. It is about the speed He walked when He was on this earth. If I don't want to get ahead of Him and find myself in a dark spot, I need to slow down and enjoy family, eating, talking, reading, working, traveling, and gazing at His beauty in His word. The world says, "Rush! Hurry! More!" There is a time for speed, but it poses the risk of missing the best scenery. I hope you enjoy this update as you reflect on His ways.
  -   Randy

One - Yes or Better

As you begin this book, we would love for you to commit to pray as you read. To that end, we thought it would be good to start by dealing with some misconceptions about prayer.

A few days before her untimely death, Janis Joplin recorded, a song that went like this: "O Lord, won't you buy me a Mercedes Benz? My friends all drive Porsches. I must make amends. Worked hard all my lifetime, no help from my friends, so oh Lord, won't you buy me a Mercedes Benz?" If you have heard it, I am sure Joplin's raspy voice, belting it out acapella, is now back in your head, as you recall the next part of the song, "Oh Lord, won't you buy me a color TV?" They really are creative prayer lyrics but not prone to be answered in the affirmative. Joplin knew that. So what type of prayer would get a "Yes!" from the Almighty?

Questions about prayer abound: What should I pray for? Why are my prayers not answered? How come I never have a desire to pray? Some people even ask, "If God knows everything, why should we pray at all?" Good questions.

Have you ever thought that perhaps part of His plan requires prayer? Now our prayers are not the initial cause of His actions but they do cause Him to act. Because of His character, He must respond when we pray. In other words, He cannot have a "Nobody Home" sign on His door. So the real question is, "How will He answer?" Now get this: as odd as it first may sound, He will answer one of two ways to the person who calls on Him in faith: Yes or Better. The challenge is seeing that if the answer is not yes, it is better.

Think about this: Jesus says He is not going to give us a stone if we ask for bread. He will do right by us. Through His perfect knowledge of what is best for us, He will direct, and decide perfectly. He loves His people and He always does what is best for them, in accordance with His glory.

So, as you start this reader and as you enter into this season, we encourage you to pray. Start with some adoration and then maybe a little confession. Next, you might want to move along to some thanksgiving. We can all park there for a while. Then you may want to wind up by asking for what you think has value. Be confident that God will say Yes or Better.

C.S. Lewis once said that he was glad God had not answered yes to many of his prayers. God had better in mind, and, over time, Lewis could look back and see that, in fact, that was indeed the case.

Daniel 9 | Nehemiah 9 | Ezra 9

Daniel 9:17-19

"Now, therefore, O our God, listen to the prayer of your servant and to his pleas for mercy, and for your own sake, O Lord, make your face to shine upon your sanctuary, which is desolate. O my God, incline your ear and hear. Open your eyes and see our desolations, and the city that is called by your name. For we do not present our pleas before you because of our righteousness, but because of your great mercy. O Lord, hear; O Lord, forgive. O Lord, pay attention and act. Delay not, for your own sake, O my God, because your city and your people are called by your name.".

_____
_____
_____
_____
_____
_____
_____
_____
_____
_____
_____
_____
_____
_____
_____
_____
_____
_____
_____

TWO – Not Because...AND!

We desired to have children. At the beginning, my husband and I were so full of hope and excitement. Since God had put the desire on both of our hearts, we just knew that it would happen, and soon!

It did not. Months turned into years. Hope glimmered only to be squashed. For nearly 8 years, my husband and I struggled with the unfulfilled desire for children, both through infertility and then in the adoption process. I admit that, over time, hope became hard to hold on to. During a particularly hard season, I felt the pain might crush me, and I worried that I might become bitter in the process. But God, being rich in His mercy, gave me strength and peace that was beyond comprehension.

You know that verse about God not giving you more than you can handle? I used to say to my husband that God had far too high an opinion of me because I couldn't handle it. But that's really the point, isn't it? If God only gave us what we could handle, there would be no need for a Savior. The truth is, what I can handle is almost nothing. But God can and did give me strength to endure, and He deepened my faith in the process.

So He taught me to wait. And in the waiting, He taught me to repeat to myself through prayer, speaking out loud, and journaling the truths of God found in His word. "The Lord is Good. The Lord is my Rock and my Fortress. His Love Endures Forever." By His grace, I chose to praise Him even in difficult times. When I didn't feel it, I repeated the Truth, even more to keep it hidden in my heart.

After 7 ½ years of waiting, the Lord answered our prayer with a YES! We had the amazing privilege of adopting our son and 5 ½ years later, our daughter. There is no question in our hearts that this was from the Lord; you could see His fingerprints in the smallest details surrounding their adoptions. The celebration of family and friends has been wonderful, and there have been so many shouts of "God is Good!" and He is. Our children are a gift from God.

God is good, but I don't want to forget this important truth. God isn't good BECAUSE he granted the desire of our hearts. He is good - AND in His great love and mercy towards us, He blessed us with children. This is the truth that I must hold close to my heart. God owes me nothing, AND yet He has chosen to grant me the desire of my heart. That may be the best lesson I can learn as my husband, and I parent our son and daughter.

Maybe you are struggling with unfulfilled desires. I doubt that reading this will take the pain away, but I hope that it offers encouragement. That you might look to Him and His word for comfort in your time of distress. Speak to others who have hope for you. Pray. And perhaps, as I found, you will be able to say to yourself, "[Even, and maybe especially, in my unfulfilled desire I] praise God from whom all blessings flow."

2 Samuel 7:28 | Psalm 107 | 1 Thessalonians 5:18

2 Samuel 7:28
Sovereign Lord, you are God! Your covenant is trustworthy, and you have promised these good things to your servant.

Psalm 107:1-2a
"Give thanks to the Lord for He is good, His love endures forever. Let the redeemed of the Lord tell their story."

1 Thessalonians 5:18
"Give thanks in all circumstances; for this is God's will for you in Christ Jesus."

_____
_____
_____
_____
_____
_____
_____

Three – More Than A Day of Thanksgiving

Bradford, Washington, and Lincoln thought we, as Americans, needed to be spurred on to gratitude, and each, in turn, wrote a proclamation calling for a day of thanksgiving. They were leaders who looked at the landscape and saw that there was much for which to be thankful. In fact, they felt so strongly about it that they made it a national event.

We have just experienced that holiday, institutionalized as Thanksgiving Day. How did we do? For what were we thankful, and how did we express it? My guess is most of us prayed a prayer of thanksgiving at the meal where our families and friends gathered together while the turkey, mashed potatoes, gravy, pumpkin pie, and lots of other high-fat food waited to be consumed. A thanksgiving prayer is a good place to start.

After dinner, some of us watched a little football on TV, took an afternoon nap, and maybe even a short walk to "work off the calories." We may have expressed some thanks for the time of rest and enjoyment. That was the right second step.

Now may be time for the third step. Thanksgiving is not over. The Apostle Paul wrote, "Be joyful always, pray continually, give thanks in all circumstances, for this is God's will for you in Christ Jesus" (1 Thessalonians 5:18). Give thanks in all circumstances - that includes weekdays.

The Pilgrims may have recalled Paul's words after their disastrous first year in the new world. They were people who did not have a day of thanksgiving; they strived to live lives of thanksgiving. They were followers of Christ, who had come to a hard place for freedom, and they nearly died in the process. That is why they were specifically thanking God; for life in Christ. Washington and Lincoln also were thanking God for specific events, but they were not saying that a single day was sufficient and that we should quickly move on to the Christmas shopping season.

All of these men were calling people to a life of thanksgiving in whatever circumstances. Thanksgiving Day is just a starting, or better, a re-starting point to a life of remembering our Creator and blessing Him daily, even hourly, for His common grace and His favor to us as His people. That is the heart of Thanksgiving. We encourage you, as you head back to shopping and life, to think of how you can be thankful because the circumstances could be intriguing for you and your family this season. They may even be hard. How might you do that? Paul gives us a clue, after telling us it is God's will for us to be thankful, when he says, "...in Christ Jesus." It is His birth we will now celebrate as we await His return. In Him and through Him, we can be thankful.

Psalm 147:7 | Colossians 3:16 |Hebrews 12:28

Psalm 147:7
"Sing to the Lord with thanksgiving; make melody to our God on the lyre!"

Colossians 3:16
"Let the word of Christ dwell in you richly, teaching and admonishing one another in all wisdom, singing psalms and hymns and spiritual songs, with thankfulness in your hearts to God."

Hebrews 12:28
"Therefore let us be grateful for receiving a kingdom that cannot be shaken, and thus let us offer to God acceptable worship, with reverence and awe,"

_____
_____
_____
_____
_____
_____
_____
_____
_____
_____
_____
_____
_____

Four – Thankful Pumpkins

My son loves pumpkins. He eagerly looks forward to going to the pumpkin patch, and then once they are home, he hugs the big ones and puts the small ones in his dump truck, making the most of every minute that we have them. I convinced him that if we didn't carve them, they would last longer - which is true, and also less messy - so ours typically last until Thanksgiving.

A few years ago, I heard someone talk about the idea of a "thankful pumpkin". The idea is that you would take a marker and write out things that you are thankful for, scrolling around and all over the pumpkin. We tried it and loved it, so it is now a tradition. My children are still very young, so our list of things we are thankful for is kind of all over the map – friends, church, chocolate, gravity, sports, God's Grace (we are also learning the catechism), the list goes on and on. In a time of year that can be so much about getting and rushing, I love this tradition of slowing down to physically write down things that we are thankful for, both the big and the small things, and I love that we do it every day in November – or at least most days. It's good for my heart, and I hope that it is instilling in my children a practice of slowing down and giving thanks to the Lord.

As you are likely reading this in late November, you may not have any pumpkins sitting around, but you can still give it a try. Today, write down five things you are thankful for, tomorrow write five more, ask the Lord to open your eyes and your heart to see His grace and mercy in your life, and then give Him thanks for it. I hope that this is a blessing to you this Thanksgiving season.

Psalm 9:1-2 | Psalm 100:3-5 | 1 Thessalonians 5:18

Psalm 9:1-2
I will give thanks to you, Lord, with all my heart;
  I will tell of all your wonderful deeds.
I will be glad and rejoice in you;
  I will sing the praises of your name, O Most High.

Psalm 100:3-5

Know that the Lord is God.
*   It is he who made us, and we are his;*
*   we are his people, the sheep of his pasture.*
Enter his gates with thanksgiving
*   and his courts with praise;*
*   give thanks to him and praise his name.*
For the Lord is good and his love endures forever;
*   his faithfulness continues through all generations.*

Five - A Humble Prayer by Philip Doddridge
(modernized by R Schlichting)

He was a contemporary of Isaac Watts and George Whitefield; one of those 18th-century men that God used to shape the church. He was a theologian, an educator, and a man of prayer.

We thought it might be helpful for you to pray a prayer written by him. And perhaps you might begin to write some of your prayers as the Lord prompts. Here you go:

> *"Blessed God! I sincerely acknowledge before you my own weakness and insufficiency to begin anything that is spiritually good. I have failed a thousand times; and yet my foolish heart would again 'trust itself,' (Prov. 28:26) and form resolutions in its own strength. So, I ask that this be the first fruit of your gracious influence upon my heart: to bring it to a humble distrust of itself and to a rest in you! I rejoice, O Lord, in the kind assurances, which you give me of your readiness to bestow liberally and richly so great a benefit to my heart. I do, therefore, according to your condescending invitation, come with boldness to your throne, that I may find grace to help in every time of need. (Heb. 4:16)*
>
> *I mean not, O Lord God, to turn your grace into a license for immorality or perverseness or to make my weakness an excuse for negligence and sloth. I confess that you have already given me more strength than I have used! I charge it upon myself, and not on you, that I have even recently received still more grace from you through your Word and the Spirit. I desire for the future to be found diligent in the use of all appointed means of grace. When I neglect the grace you have given me, petitions like these become a profane mockery, and they might even provoke you to take away what I have, rather than prevail upon you to give me more. But firmly resolving to exert myself to the utmost to use the grace you have given, I earnestly ask for more grace, that I may be enabled to fulfill that resolution. Be surety, O Lord, to me your servant for good. (Psa. 119:122) Be pleased to shed your sanctifying influences on my soul, to*

form me for every duty you require. Implant, I ask you, grace and virtue deep in my heart. Bear with me in the midst of me foolishly assaulting your grace. I know I will continue from time to time to do that while I am still in this world and carry about with me so much sin.

Fill me with good affections towards you, my God, and towards my fellow-creatures. Remind me always of your presence, and may I remember that every secret sentiment of my soul is open to you. May I, therefore, guard against the first risings of sin, and the first approaches to it. May I guard that Satan may not find room for his evil suggestions. I earnestly beg that you Lord, would fill my heart with your Holy Spirit. Dwell in me, and walk with me, and let my body be the temple of the Holy Ghost.

May I be so joined to Jesus my Lord, as to be one with him, (1 Cor. 6:17) and feel His invigorating influences continually bearing me on, superior to every temptation and to every corruption. So that while young people shall faint and grow weary, I may so wait upon the Lord as to renew my strength, (Isaiah 40:30,31) and may go on from one degree of faith, and love, and zeal, and holiness, to another.

Six – Thanks

Have you ever wondered why some people love Thanksgiving so much? I have talked to many people who say that they enjoy Thanksgiving more than Christmas because it is less focused on what we get and more on what we have been given. In a way, that sounds strange because giving and receiving gifts can be enjoyable. However, without a thankful heart, gifts may eventually reveal their natural essence: they are just things and cannot satisfy. No doubt, God wants us to have a thankful heart. Our problem is that in our fast-paced lives, we rarely stop and focus our hearts towards the One to whom we should be eternally grateful. So how can we stop long enough to feast on what is good for our souls? Thanksgiving!

In my family, we all gather in the kitchen before Thanksgiving dinner. We go around, and everyone shares something that they are thankful for. It is a special time to celebrate and give thanks for the blessings that each of us has experienced over the past year. Some of the things are simple, and some are profound.

Now, lest you think that I happen to have the perfect family that always gets what we want, let me assure you that we have had some challenging times. And we have had to learn to be thankful, even for the sad things. That can be really difficult to do. Sometimes we can see that struggles brought us something wonderful in return; other times, there is no obvious reason or blessing that is accompanying hardship – it is just hard. So this year, once again, I join with you as we learn that no matter how trying the past year has been, there is something that we can find to be thankful about: even if it is simply the fact that we have the common graces of air, eyesight, hearing, some health, a roof over our heads, food to eat, and some friends.

I hope that is helpful. It is good and healthy to spend extended time in thanksgiving once a year, but we don't need to wait until the leaves turn golden and the weather turns cool to have a thankful heart. How would our lives be different if we chose to be truly thankful all through the year and stopped to thank the Lord on a regular basis for His blessings? I think we know we would be happier, more contented people. It doesn't have to be a big sweeping event every day. It could be a short and simple prayer of thankfulness, daily re-focusing our lives on the things above. A small habit could result in big-time heart change. So what is stopping us? Us. We have a tendency to look on the dark side, and it drags us down. That is no way to live. So, can I encourage you to start a new habit? Think of one thing to be thankful for each day. Write it down, share it with a friend, and pray it back to God. That could promote a spirit of gratitude that would be contagious.

Isaiah 12:4 | 2 Corinthians 4:14-16 | Colossians 3:14-16

Isaiah 12:4
"And you will say in that day: "Give thanks to the Lord, call upon his name, make known his deeds among the peoples, proclaim that his name is exalted."

2 Corinthians 4:14-16
"Knowing that He who raised the Lord Jesus will raise us also with Jesus and bring us with you into his presence. For it is all for your sake, so that as grace extends to more and more people it may increase thanksgiving, to the glory of God. So we do not lose heart. Though our outer self is wasting away, our inner self is being renewed day by day."

_____
_____
_____
_____
_____
_____
_____
_____
_____
_____
_____
_____
_____

Seven - The Coming of A King

I remember being around 7 years old when my uncle took me out for the day. It was in   the very early days of the 1960s. I do not recall him saying where we were going. But we ended up at a place swarming with excited people. The crowd lined the road on both sides. I do not remember the specific details, but I recall the crowd all looking in one direction and someone saying, "Here he comes!" It was the President of the United States.

I think I caught a glimpse of him as his motorcade sped by, but what I most remember was the crowd. How they cheered and how they waved. The excitement was electric and tangible. I felt it, and I knew that the man in that car was honored, loved, and respected. After he passed by, the crowd dispersed, satisfied that they had caught just a glimpse of him.

Daniel saw the Lord coming towards the Ancient of Days, and all power, glory, honor, and rule was given to Him. Moses caught a glimpse too, as did Abraham and others. When we worship together, He is in our midst. Not being able to physically see Him does not matter. The King has come, is coming, and will come again. I pray that as you worship corporately during this Christmas season, you would sense the Lord is with you and that He is worthy of honor, love, respect, and more. And when you leave that you would say you had caught just a glimpse, and were satisfied.

Psalm 145:12-14 | Daniel 12:5-13 | Isaiah 37:15-17

Psalm 145:-14
to make known to the children of man your mighty deeds,
  and the glorious splendor of your kingdom.
Your kingdom is an everlasting kingdom,
  and your dominion endures throughout all generations.
[The Lord is faithful in all his words
  and kind in all his works.]
The Lord upholds all who are falling
  and raises up all who are bowed down.

Isaiah 6:1-3

In the year that King Uzziah died I saw the Lord sitting upon a throne, high and lifted up; and the train of his robe filled the temple. Above him stood the seraphim. Each had six wings: with two he covered his face, and with two he covered his feet, and with two he flew. And one called to another and said: "Holy, holy, holy is the Lord of hosts; the whole earth is full of his glory!"

Isaiah 37:15-17

And Hezekiah prayed to the Lord: "O Lord of hosts, God of Israel, enthroned above the cherubim, you are the God, you alone, of all the kingdoms of the earth; you have made heaven and earth. Incline your ear, O Lord, and hear; open your eyes, O Lord, and see; and hear all the words of Sennacherib, which he has sent to mock the living God.

Eight - Golden Gift Box

I love Christmas and all that comes with it. I love Santa, Frosty and Rudolph; giving gifts and holiday parties; all the secular parts of Christmas that really have nothing to do with the true meaning of Christmas. They can be really enjoyable and, I believe are in and of themselves are not a bad thing. But if we let them become a distraction from the real thing, then we are missing the point.

Growing up, we had a 'golden gift box'. It was the first gift put under the tree, and it was the first present that my sister and I opened every year on Christmas Eve. Inside, my mom had created a set of visual cues to remind us of our Savior and why we celebrate His birth. There was a small golden teapot to represent our blessings that are poured out, golden joy bells, and a set of baby toy keys spray painted gold to represent the keys to the kingdom. There was also a tiny Lamb's book of life where our names are written, a light bulb to represent Jesus as the light of the world, a cross for our salvation, a dove of peace, and broken chains to represent our broken chain of sins - which Jesus did on the cross. Because of His great love for us, He had to come to earth, take on flesh, live and die, to save us.

We went through the box every year, and I am sure that there were years where we thought, "Yeah, mom, okay, now how about the real presents?" But we always went through it slowly, talking through the items and what each meant to us. We talked about how Jesus was the "ultimate gift" and that the presents we give each other are supposed to serve as a reminder of our ultimate gift in Christ.

As I have grown older, I am so thankful for traditions like that. Now, as an adult, I have a golden gift box at my house, too - although mine is actually silver because that matches my Christmas decorations better. I love carrying on the tradition with my children. Every time I see that box, I am reminded that the greatest gift I receive at Christmas is Jesus and His gift of salvation. Do you have any Christmas traditions that point you to our Savior

King who came to earth to save us? If not, maybe this is the year to start one. Maybe you'll create a golden gift box or an advent wreath, or who knows; you may be more creative than any of us. By all means, enjoy the Christmas season and all that it entails but don't forget to find time to focus on the true significance of Christmas.

Matthew 2 | Romans 5:1-8 | Romans 6:23

Romans 5:1-8

Therefore, since we have been justified through faith, we have peace with God through our Lord Jesus Christ, 2 through whom we have gained access by faith into this grace in which we now stand. And we boast in the hope of the glory of God. Not only so, but we also glory in our sufferings, because we know that suffering produces perseverance; perseverance, character; and character, hope. And hope does not put us to shame, because God's love has been poured out into our hearts through the Holy Spirit, who has been given to us.

You see, at just the right time, when we were still powerless, Christ died for the ungodly. Very rarely will anyone die for a righteous person, though for a good person someone might possibly dare to die. But God demonstrates his own love for us in this: While we were still sinners, Christ died for us.

Romans 6:23

For the wages of sin is death, but the gracious gift of God is eternal life in Christ Jesus our Lord.

_____
_____
_____
_____
_____
_____
_____
_____
_____
_____
_____
_____

Nine – Supply Chain

Every year there are supply chain issues during the holidays. In recent years, it has been perhaps a bit worse. There are a lot of reasons for the situation, but the bottom line is that goods and supplies cannot get where they are supposed to go. In many cases, vendors have purchased and paid for the goods, but they cannot get them. In the meantime, prices go up because demand is up, and supplies are short. That is the classic economic theory at work.

We can hope that eventually, the chain will get fixed, ships will move, and cargo will be unloaded. In the meantime, we wait because there is nothing we as individuals can do about it. Some have predicted that Christmas toys may be short. The shelves may be a bit bare. That may cause panic buying. What a vicious cycle!

Here is the good news. Our supply as Christians is never delayed. It is not stuck on a ship. It does not need to be unloaded. We can avail ourselves of the power of God anytime and anywhere. He is always ready to meet with us and give us the supply that we need. He will give us Him. As we begin the Christmas season, maybe you or a loved one will not get a gift because it is "out of stock," but please know that you have treasure in Him - and He gives us the Best Gifts:

> **Peace** – "Peace I leave with you; my peace I give to you. Not as the world gives do I give to you. Let not your hearts be troubled, neither let them be afraid." John 14:27

> **Rest** – "Come to Me, all who are weary and burdened, and I will give you rest." Matthew 11:28

> **Hope** - "Now may the God of hope fill you with all joy and peace in believing, so that you will abound in hope by the power of the Holy Spirit." Romans 15:13
> He is the gift, and He wants to supply all your needs in Christ Jesus.

Philippians 4:19
And my God shall supply all your need according to His riches in glory by Christ Jesus.

2 Corinthians 9:8
And God is able to make all grace abound to you, so that having all sufficiency in all things at all times, you may abound in every good work.

Romans 8: 32
He who did not spare His own Son, but delivered Him over for us all, how will He not also with Him freely give us all things?

2 Corinthians 4:7
But we have this treasure in earthen vessels, so that the surpassing greatness of the power will be of God and not from ourselves.

_____
_____
_____
_____
_____
_____
_____
_____
_____
_____
_____
_____
_____
_____
_____
_____
_____
_____
_____
_____
_____
_____
_____

Ten - Instead of Sheep

"...I count my blessings instead of sheep. And I fall asleep counting my blessings."
- *Count Your Blessings, White Christmas,*
Irving Berlin, 1954

It is an Oscar-nominated song from one of my favorite Christmas movies of all time, White Christmas. In the movie, Rosemary Clooney's character is worried about everything under the sun and as a result, she can't sleep. Bing Crosby's character, suggests that instead of thinking about the things that trouble her that she think about all the blessings that she has instead.

In a way, this reminds me of the story of Mary and Martha when Jesus came to visit. Stay with me here, Martha was busy thinking about all the things that had to be done and busily worked in the kitchen. Mary recognized the blessing of having Jesus in her home and took the opportunity to sit at his feet and listen to him. She let the world fade away, and the only thing that she was focused on was Him. Maybe you are saying, "Hey, wait a minute, there are things that need to get done during the holidays. Are you suggesting that we just ignore responsibilities?" Well, yes and no. No, I am not suggesting that you completely ignore responsibilities and things that have to get done. But yes, I am suggesting that it may be appropriate from time to time to stop the rushing and rest.

With all of the Christmas cards, holiday parties, and gifts to buy, have you found yourself running on empty or feeling that you are missing the blessing of the holiday season? Do you get lost in the busy nature of the Christmas season or really just life in general, forgetting that we can and need to come and rest at the feet of Jesus? I know I often do. When was the last time you stopped what you were doing in the midst of stress and worries and sought rest in Him? Are you Mary, Martha, or somewhere in between?

Can I encourage you to try today, even just for a few minutes, to stop, let the worries of the day fade, and meet with Jesus? We'll do it together. Whether sleep is evading you or not, if you stop and spend   time dwelling on the Lord and His great love for us, it will be a blessing at any time of year but especially in the busy holiday season.

Psalm 21 | Psalm 94 | Proverbs 12:25 | Ephesians 1

Proverbs 12:25
Anxiety in a man's heart weighs him down, but a good word makes him glad.

Ephesians 1:15-23
For this reason, because I have heard of your faith in the Lord Jesus and your love toward all the saints, I do not cease to give thanks for you, remembering you in my prayers, that the God of our Lord Jesus Christ, the Father of glory, may give you the Spirit of wisdom and of revelation in the knowledge of him, having the eyes of your hearts enlightened, that you may know what is the hope to which he has called you, what are the riches of his glorious inheritance in the saints, and what is the immeasurable greatness of his power toward us who believe, according to the working of his great might that he worked in Christ when he raised him from the dead and seated him at his right hand in the heavenly places, far above all rule and authority and power and dominion, and above every name that is named, not only in this age but also in the one to come. And he put all things under his feet and gave him as head over all things to the church, which is his body, the fullness of him who fills all in all."

Eleven - Shopping Days

So how many shopping days are left? Sorry to stress you out. Or maybe now is the time to get stressed out! Who will you buy for? From where will the money come? When will you get the decorations on the house? Where will you have Christmas dinner? Will you have anyone with whom to share it? Will you be invited to anyone's home? Will you be alone on Christmas day? Those questions are crazy, aren't they? It should not be this way, but it is. Christmas is a hectic season that seems to get longer and more intense each year.

Can we offer a few thoughts and maybe some suggestions? They may have been said before, but they may be new to you. We thought this would be the time to say, "Peace to all those who stress out over Christmas!" and give you a few pointers:

Memorize three words and say them to yourself when you get in your car, and turn the ignition switch each day between now and Dec. 24th. Here they are, "Jesus started this." By "this," we do not mean the Christmas holiday. We mean all of this. Through Him, all things were created. He came to save us from our sin. As you start the car, try to remember, "Jesus started this." That may move you towards thinking, praising, and other good things.

Think about this as you pull out your credit or debit card to buy a gift. In fact, you could write it and tape it to your card. "Jesus purchased redemption." He bought the souls of mankind on the cross of Calvary. Corny? Maybe it is. But is it helpful to your soul as a reminder? Try it.

If you are old-fashioned and write checks or pay with cash, perhaps you could be reminded as you pay for purchases that, "Jesus paid it all." He paid for every sin of those He loves. It is the "why" of Christmas.

As you think about with whom you will spend Christmas, perhaps you would remember the number "3." The fellowship of the

Trinity: the Father giving the Son, the Son sacrificing for His friends, and the Spirit moving to change hearts.

I am sure you can think of many other ways that you can shift the focus to Jesus. From past personal failure, we can tell you that it is hard to do. A plan can be helpful, if you lay it out early. Then you can then enjoy the season, being grounded in your faith, washing your mind with the water of the word as you traverse over the valley and through the woods to grandmother's house.

Psalm 29 | John 14:26-28 | Jude 1:2

Psalm 29: 10-11
The Lord sits enthroned over the flood;
the Lord sits enthroned as king forever.
May the Lord give strength to his people!
May the Lord bless his people with peace!

John 14:26-28
But the Helper, the Holy Spirit, whom the Father will send in my name, he will teach you all things and bring to your remembrance all that I have said to you. Peace I leave with you; my peace I give to you. Not as the world gives do I give to you. Let not your hearts be troubled, neither let them be afraid. You heard me say to you, 'I am going away, and I will come to you.' If you loved me, you would have rejoiced, because I am going to the Father, for the Father is greater than I.

Jude 1:2
"May mercy, peace, and love be multiplied to you."

_____
_____
_____
_____
_____
_____
_____
_____
_____

Twelve – Candles

I don't know anyone who hates candles. They are warm and inviting. Sometimes they smell good too. They are passive, but with a hint of danger. People like candles, and many have them in their house this time of year. Some people even put fake candles in their windows! Candles are everywhere.

A few people have five of them on their dinner table. The Advent wreath is an ancient tradition. You may have seen one before; it is a round flat wreath with three purple candles, one pink candle, and a white candle in the middle.

The interesting thing about these candles is that they are not all lit at the same time. One candle is lit for the first Sunday of Advent, and the next week, two candles are lit. By week four, all the candles are burning brightly. The fifth candle is lit on Christmas Eve.

So what is the story? Well, there are several stories, as it turns out, because the tradition goes back a long way. Most common is that the candles are lit to prepare us and to call us to wait. Prepare for what? Prepare our hearts for Jesus. Wait for what? Wait for Him to return. The Bible is full of candles and waiting. As Christians, we are called to look to the past with great joy and the future with great hope in spite of our circumstances. The light of the world descended into darkness and He will come again.

Now a few details: The first candle is the candle of prophecy; the prophets said he would come and we say He will come back again. The second candle is the candle of love. His love is everlasting, and we are called to love others as He has loved us. Third is the candle of joy. He suffered greatly for the joy set before Him, so that our joy may be made complete. The fourth is peace. He made peace for us with God, and we should be peacemakers.

Of course, the center candle, the Christ candle, represents the light of the world coming to chase away all darkness. He is the center of all things.

So you might want to experiment having an advent wreath. There is no magic to it. It is just a tool designed to help us focus on the One who came to save His people from their sin.

Malachi 3:1-5 | Luke 1

Malachi 3:1-5

"Behold, I send my messenger, and he will prepare the way before me. And the Lord whom you seek will suddenly come to his temple; and the messenger of the covenant in whom you delight, behold, he is coming, says the Lord of hosts. But who can endure the day of his coming, and who can stand when he appears? For he is like a refiner's fire and like fullers' soap. He will sit as a refiner and purifier of silver, and he will purify the sons of Levi and refine them like gold and silver, and they will bring offerings in righteousness to the Lord. Then the offering of Judah and Jerusalem will be pleasing to the Lord as in the days of old and as in former years. Then I will draw near to you for judgment. I will be a swift witness against the sorcerers, against the adulterers, against those who swear falsely, against those who oppress the hired worker in his wages, the widow and the fatherless, against those who thrust aside the sojourner, and do not fear me, says the Lord of hosts."

_____

_____

_____

_____

_____

_____

_____

_____

_____

_____

_____

_____

_____

_____

_____

_____

_____

_____

Thirteen - O Antiphons

As G.K.Chesterton once said, "Tradition is the democracy of the dead. It is gives votes to the most obscure of all classes; those who have gone before us."

The Benedictines went before us, and we want to take a moment to count their votes to see if we might have a majority on this topic. They introduced the O Antiphons to the church as a series of sayings to be used during the Advent season. We thought you might enjoy using them during family devotions this month.

Our ancestors have overwhelmingly said Christmas is a time to hold fast to the deep mystery of what happened and look forward to the mystery of what is to come.

The monks arranged these antiphons with a definite purpose. If one starts with the last title and takes the first letter of each one - Emmanuel, Rex, Oriens, Clavis, Radix, Adonai, Sapientia - the Latin words Ere Cras are formed. It means, "Tomorrow, I will come." Therefore, the Lord Jesus, whose coming we have prepared for in Advent, and whom we have addressed in these seven Messianic titles, "speaks" to us saying, "Tomorrow, I will come." This is, indeed, our hope. All of the prophecies are from Isaiah. We encourage you to go back and read the originals; maybe take one each day this week to meditate on them.

O Sapientia (Wisdom):
"The spirit of the Lord shall rest upon him: a spirit of wisdom and of understanding, a spirit of counsel and of strength, a spirit of knowledge and fear of the Lord, and his delight shall be the fear of the Lord." (Isaiah 11:2-3)

O Adonai (Lord):
"The Lord is Our King; it is He who will save us." (Isaiah 33:22)

O Radix Jesse (Root):
"But a shoot shall sprout from the stump of Jesse, and from his roots

a bud shall blossom." (Isaiah 11:1)

O Clavis David (Key):

"I will place the Key of the House of David on His shoulder; when he opens, no one will shut, when he shuts, no one will open." (Isaiah 22:22)

O Oriens (Light):

"The people who walked in darkness have seen a great light; upon those who dwelt in the land of gloom a light has shown." (Isaiah 9:2)

O Rex Gentium (King of nations):

"For a child is born to us, a son is given us; and the government shall be upon His shoulders and he will be called Wonderful Counselor, Mighty God." (Isaiah 9:6)

O Emmanuel (God with us):

"The Lord himself will give you this sign: the Virgin shall be with child, and bear a son, and shall name him Emmanuel." (Isaiah 7:14)

Fourteen – Striving for the Perfect Christmas

We are striving for perfection, to make everything (at least look) okay. This year will be the perfect Christmas: we'll take beautiful Christmas photos, everyone will get along, and the whole holiday season will be like a Norman Rockwell painting from start to finish. The truth is that nothing is ever perfect, and the more that we push to make everything look perfect, the less peace and enjoyment we will actually have.

Remember the first Christmas? I'm betting that was not the way that Mary and Joseph had planned for the birth of their child to go. Instead of a nice, clean, warm home, they were in a strange place, sleeping in a barn. She had to put her baby in a feeding trough. Not my idea of how I'd want it to go, and yet in Luke 2:19, it says, "But Mary treasured up all these things and pondered them in her heart." If she can treasure those crazy things, then we can probably handle a Christmas card where not everyone's looking at the camera or burned turkey or whatever goes wrong with your holiday.

This isn't to say that we can't try to make our houses look nice or desire and try to take a nice family photo, but if we allow those things to steal our joy or try to make them the sole focus of the holidays we'll miss it.

Since we can't do everything, maybe it would help to make a priority list of the things that are really important to you. You may find that some of the things you stress the most about don't actually matter to you, and you can just not do them this year. Maybe this is the year you focus on a few really special things and enjoy them to the fullest, and the rest either happen or don't happen, but you won't spend the whole season stressing about it.

Make peace your number one priority this season. - not manufactured peace, not new-age inner peace that you control, but real, true peace that comes from Jesus Christ our Savior. His peace passes all human understanding. If you let it guide your heart and mind this season, you may find that it rubs off on those around you too.

Numbers 6:24-26 | Luke 2 | John 14:26-28

Numbers 6:24-26
The Lord bless you
and keep you;
the Lord make his face shine on you
and be gracious to you;
the Lord turn his face toward you
and give you peace

John 14:26-28
But the Advocate, the Holy Spirit, whom the Father will send in my name, will teach you all things and will remind you of everything I have said to you. Peace I leave with you; my peace I give you. I do not give to you as the world gives. Do not let your hearts be troubled and do not be afraid.
"You heard me say, 'I am going away and I am coming back to you.' If you loved me, you would be glad that I am going to the Father, for the Father is greater than I.

_____
_____
_____
_____
_____
_____
_____
_____
_____
_____
_____
_____
_____
_____
_____
_____
_____
_____
_____
_____

Fifteen - Christmas Music

Truth be told, some of you are not fans of Christmas music played on the radio. I know it is hard to tell your friends and family, so we can keep it as our secret. That song about the shoes really grates on your nerves doesn't it? Those Chipmunks could drive anyone up a wall. Where is your pellet gun when you need it? Bruce Springsteen should stick to rock and roll. And baby, it is not that cold outside!

Now for others of you, who read the last paragraph in shock, not believing anyone could be a Christmas music hater, there is nothing like Nat King Cole, Tran Siberian Orchestra or Burl Ives. Further, that little boy loved his mother and wanted to get her those shoes as a sign of his affection! As far as you are concerned, holly, jolly Christmas music should start in October and run through January, right?

I am not going to take sides, but I do want to ask us all to consider going deep. Jingle Bells may be upbeat and White Christmas nostalgic, but the words written by the great Christian hymn writers touch something deeper in our souls as we reflect on the event and the events to come.

So, as we enter into the season of carols, can we encourage you to think about the context in which the great hymns were written? Many of our carols were written by men and women who were passionate about the work of Christ in the world. Frank Houghton, who wrote *Thou Who Wast Rich Beyond All Splendor*, wrote it in response to the persecution of Christians in China. Isaac Watts knew as he wrote *Joy to the World* that God "ruled the world with truth and grace and made the nations prove the glories of His righteousness" because of his personal experience.

Imagine the priest who wrote *Silent Night*, starring up at the sky and seeing the beauty of God in creation; the unknown author of *O Come, O Come Emmanuel* longing for the second coming, or Charles Wesley remembering his own conversion as he penned,

"God and sinners reconciled!"

Now maybe you might take a moment and sing, yes, sing these Christmas hymns; as the words soak into your soul. Then you can look for more.

O Come O Come Emmanuel (author unknown)
"O come, Thou Rod of Jesse, free Thine own from Satan's tyranny
From depths of Hell Thy people save and give them victory o'er the
grave Rejoice! Rejoice! Emmanuel shall come to thee, O Israel."

Angels From The Realms of Glory (James Montgomery)
"Saints before the altar bending, watching long in hope and fear,
Suddenly the Lord, descending, In His temple shall appear:
Come and worship, Come and worship, worship Christ, the newborn
King!"

Matthew 1:22-24 | Luke 2:12-14

Matthew 1:22-24
Now all this took place so that what was spoken by the Lord through the
prophet would be fulfilled: "Behold, the virgin will conceive and give birth
to a Son, and they shall name Him Immanuel," which translated means,
"God with us." And Joseph awoke from his sleep and did as the angel of the
Lord commanded him, and took Mary as his wife.

Luke 2:12-14
And this will be a sign for you: you will find a baby wrapped in swaddling
cloths and lying in a manger." And suddenly there was with the angel a
multitude of the heavenly host praising God and saying, "Glory to God in
the highest, and on earth peace among those with whom he is pleased!"

_____
_____
_____
_____
_____
_____
_____
_____

Sixteen - Did You Like It? Good it's a Tradition!

Every year for as long as I can remember, we have decorated our Christmas tree listening to Bing Crosby and then Motown Christmas. We have always had plenty of different Christmas music, but we never even thought about playing anything else while putting up the tree. To this day, any time that I hear "That Christmas Feeling" by Bing Crosby, I am taken back to my parent's living room - Christmas lights and ornaments with a warm nostalgic glow. I love that, I love those memories, and I love that I have those traditions.

Growing up, we had lots of traditions. We used to joke that if we did it once and liked it, it was a tradition. If we didn't, well, then it was just something we did that one time. Another of my favorite traditions is the annual Christmas party with my mom's sisters and their husbands and kids. Every year at the beginning of the season, we would go to my aunt's house, and we'd play or decorate Christmas cookies or whatever we decided was fun until it was time for dinner. Then we'd eat and go down to the family room to open presents. We always had Christmas PJs or matching t-shirts from our grandmother. Our Mawmaw always made sure she found or made some kind of matching Christmas attire for all 7 of us. Then we'd all put on the matching Christmas garb, and the kids would pile on my aunt's big blue couch for a picture. Early on, we barely took up half of the couch. These days we don't get matching Christmas clothes, but we still take a picture on the same couch, with a few sitting on the arms or in front of the couch as we are all now adults. This year we will take that picture on the newly reupholstered couch because my aunt couldn't bear to get rid of it. It is part of the tradition.

I love traditions. They seem to root us to others, bring back good memories. Most traditions have some level of enjoyment, or we would never keep doing them. We teach these traditions to those who are younger, our children, nieces, nephews, and so on, in hopes that they will carry them on for years to come. But maybe you don't have good memories from childhood or your life is such that you can't really participate in your previous traditions. It's never too late to start traditions. Decide now that you will let the past be the past, and this year you will start a new tradition - one of hope for the future.

Let us never forget that the best tradition we can have is a tradition of true faith in Christ within our families. He is the one who has given us the gift of family, whether it is the family you were born with or one you have formed over time. That gift of family is a small taste here on earth of our heavenly family.

Romans 5: 1-5 | I Corinthians 13: 4-13 | Ephesians 2

Romans 5:1-5
Therefore, since we have been justified by faith, we have peace with God through our Lord Jesus Christ. Through him we have also obtained access by faith into this grace in which we stand, and we rejoice in hope of the glory of God. Not only that, but we rejoice in our sufferings, knowing that suffering produces endurance, and endurance produces character, and character produces hope, and hope does not put us to shame, because God's love has been poured into our hearts through the Holy Spirit who has been given to us.

_____
_____
_____
_____
_____
_____
_____
_____
_____
_____
_____
_____
_____
_____
_____
_____
_____
_____
_____

Seventeen – The Word Became Flesh and Dwelt Among Us

It is a wonderful quote:

> "St John sums up the whole life and work of Jesus this way: 'The Word became flesh and dwelt among us; and we beheld his glory, glory as of the only begotten of the Father, full of grace and truth.' That, please note, is a careful re-definition of glory. When you look at the Word becoming flesh, you do not see the sort of glory that Augustus Caesar and emperors work for. You see the glory that is the family likeness of God himself. Caesar's glory is full of brute force and deep ambiguity. God's glory – Jesus glory is full of grace and truth. The royal babe in the cowshed overturns all that the human empire stands for." N.T. Wright

Man-made glory can be very shiny; but if it is not taken captive to the glory of God and if it does not point to Him, it is but tin, sure to rust. Often the glory of man has been gained by brute force and has much ambiguity as to its origins. Not so with the glory revealed in Christ Jesus. It is revealed in grace and truth.

The truth can be hard at times, can't it? You know that if you have had to share hard news with someone. The truth is that He did become flesh and dwell among us. During this season, most people do not know or believe that. So part of your holiday activity perhaps needs to be to pray for those who have not had their hearts turned to God. During this time of year, many people are open.

Next, you are perhaps being called to serve with love—no need to get your evangelism button out of the drawer and wear it on your sleeve. Let's assume they know that you are a Christian. If so, how would they expect you to act? Will you act with grace? Will you show love to the unlovable? Will you give to those in need? Yes, we are called to be gracious and giving and loving all the time, but this season is an opportunity to go above the normal and bless those who are not in the family of God.

You have beheld His glory, even as the disciples did by the fact that you have received Him. So now is the season for that glory to be evident. Winsomely share a good word, invite someone to dinner or even encourage them to come along to church for some special Christmas program.

While you are at it, don't forget those who are in the family need encouragement, too? Maybe it is a Christian who is less fortunate in some way; maybe it is someone older, or a new believer, who needs to be blessed. There are plenty of opportunities. One last thing: don't stress here. Just a little bit of grace and truth will do, as you think about the babe who overturned all things to rescue you.

Psalm 24:9-10 | Isaiah 60:1-3 | Matthew 25:30-32

Isaiah 60:1-3
Arise, shine, for your light has come,
  and the glory of the Lord has risen upon you.
For behold, darkness shall cover the earth,
  and thick darkness the peoples;
but the Lord will arise upon you,
  and his glory will be seen upon you.
And nations shall come to your light,
  and kings to the brightness of your rising.

_____
_____
_____
_____
_____
_____
_____
_____
_____
_____
_____

Eighteen – Slowing Down To Find My Rest In Him

I was given a spa gift certificate a few months ago and recently used it. One of the first things that I noticed as I walked into the spa was that the majority of the spa was in semi-darkness, dimly lit, very quiet, and everyone spoke softly. I found that it made me feel calmer and helped me to relax as I prepared for my spa service. I have taken that idea home and now try to have times where I turn off most or all of the lights and light a few candles and sit in silence or with very quiet, soft music. Christmas is a great time to do this because you can use your Christmas tree for dim light.

As I sit, I like to do two things. First, think and pray through the things that are heavy on my heart and give them to the Lord. In 1 Peter 5:7, the scripture says, "Cast all your anxiety on him because he cares for you". So I cast my cares to Him, and then I let go of them - or at least I strive to let go. Then I like to reflect on all the things in my life that I can be thankful for. It doesn't have to be huge things; it can be simple things like being thankful to have a few minutes to sit and reflect. This is a great thing to do before going to bed or at the start of the day. Take a few minutes, shut off the TV and all the noise of the world and be still. Psalm 46:9a says, "Be still, and know that I am God". I know that this is easier said than done, but just as with anything else, it gets easier every time that you try.

Here's a quick list to go through to get you started:
- Pray for things that are worrying you
- Pray for heart change where there is sin
- Thank the Lord for the blessings in your life
- Pray for eyes to see all the blessings He gives you that you have missed.

Today, why not take 5 minutes to be still and quiet and see how God moves you.

1 Chronicles 16:33-35 | Psalm 7:17 | 1 Thessalonians 5:16-24

Psalm 7:17
I will give thanks to the Lord because of his righteousness;
  I will sing the praises of the name of the Lord Most High.

1 Thessalonians 5:16-24
Rejoice always, pray continually, give thanks in all circumstances; for this is God's will for you in Christ Jesus.
Do not quench the Spirit. Do not treat prophecies with contempt but test them all; hold on to what is good, reject every kind of evil.
May God himself, the God of peace, sanctify you through and through. May your whole spirit, soul and body be kept blameless at the coming of our Lord Jesus Christ. The one who calls you is faithful, and he will do it.

Nineteen - Shake Off the Dust

Do any of the worthless idols of the nations bring rain?
Do the skies themselves send down showers? No, it is
you, O LORD our God. Therefore our hope is in you, for
you are the one who does all this. -Jeremiah 14:22

So how is the house coming along? Whether you live in an apartment or a five-bedroom house, at this time of year there is probably a bit of scenery change going on. That may mean you need to go in the basement or attic and get those decorations out. Of course, you may have to re-arrange furniture a bit in order to get everything in its place. That is where the problem is first seen. Dust!

I know there are certain places in my house that I can go, behind the couch in the den, for example, and see the dust that has accumulated. They are places that are off the beaten track. Places where I do not go often. Places where not much activity has happened. Places hidden from public view.

I ran across a comment by John Calvin in which he speaks of us having faith, but not perfect faith. To paraphrase, he says that we still have the "dust of unbelief" on our souls. When we sit idle and do not pursue the things of Christ, dust accumulates. That is a great word picture for me. Sanctification is, then, the process by which we "shake off the dust" of unbelief; not by ourselves, but by asking the Holy Spirit to blow gently.

To worship God, I must be willing to seek the dusty places and to shake them out. I can't just simply recognize them and hope for the best. I need to look for places where the dust of greed, anxiety, fear, and other idols sits and collects. It is a bit of a messy task to clean off that dust, and I know that I cannot do it in and of myself. I need Him to show me and teach me. I need Him to motivate me to look and see. And at the end of the day, He is the one who will make the change needed.

So can I ask you if you are willing to look behind the couch? I think that you might find it refreshing at the end of the day. And the Christmas decorations will look better once you get cleaned up a bit.

John 17:16-20 | 1 Thessalonians 5:23-24 | Hebrews 9:12-14

John 17:16-20
They are not of the world, just as I am not of the world. Sanctify them in the truth; your word is truth. As you sent me into the world, so I have sent them into the world. And for their sake I consecrate myself, that they also may be sanctified in truth. "I do not ask for these only, but also for those who will believe in me through their word.

1 Thessalonians 5:23-24
Now may the God of peace himself sanctify you completely, and may your whole spirit and soul and body be kept blameless at the coming of our Lord Jesus Christ. He who calls you is faithful; he will surely do it.

Twenty - When Christmas Looks Different

Last Christmas, my husband was going through brutal chemo treatments that involved 5 days in the hospital and two weeks of recovery so that he could do 5 more days. We also had a 5-year-old and a newborn. It was also the year that "everything was canceled" - Christmas was different that year for everyone. As I've said several times in this book, I love traditions, and last year some of those traditions were impossible. So instead, we focused on doing what we could. We still drove around and looked at Christmas lights – one of our favorite Christmas traditions, but it was much shorter due to the pain from the tumor. And we added new things like decorating a gingerbread house and playing Yahtzee next to the couch so Daddy could be with us but still rest. Was it the Christmas I'd always imagined and hoped for? It was not, but it was an incredibly special Christmas.

The God that split the Red Sea also sent daily manna to feed the Israelites to meet their immediate needs. After years of sending prophets who were ignored, He was silent for 400 years. He also waited for approximately 4,000 years from the original sin in the garden to send Jesus to pay the price we could never pay to save us. God's timeline is not our timeline, and His ways are not our ways.

So what does that mean for us as we walk through hard things? Do we plaster on smiles and pretend everything is okay? Saying, "I can do this. I am enough" – in case you are prone to fall into this trap, we are not enough; we need Jesus more than we'd ever care to admit, but His grace is also more immense than we ever dare to imagine. Do we say that's just way too hard and wallow in self-pity and overwhelm, mockingly saying we are "counting it all joy"? If we are honest, we probably do some of both.

"Count it all joy, my brothers, when you meet trials of various kinds"
James 1:2

Count all of this hardness... joy? How? And also, why? I think

Romans 15:13 gives us the answer, "May the God of hope fill you with all joy and peace as you trust in him, so that you may overflow with hope by the power of the Holy Spirit." Romans 15:13. I think this verse and all of the Bible is urging us to remember that in the Lord's strength, we can count even the most challenging things joy in light of His great love for us. It's not about grinning and bearing it or pretending it isn't hard. But as we acknowledge life's difficulties, we lean into the One who can, through His power, carry us through. That might look like the church and friends being the hands and feet of Jesus in your life, we were blessed beyond measure by those that came around us last year. Or it might be you meeting those needs for someone else.

In the end, Christmas isn't actually about the traditions – no matter how much I love them. Christmas is about Jesus, God the Son, coming to Earth to save us. Not because of anything we have or ever could do, but "But because of his great love for us, God, who is rich in mercy, made us alive with Christ even when we were dead in transgressions—it is by grace you have been saved." Ephesians 2:4-5. When my world looked so different last year, it was tempting to stay discouraged and overwhelmed - to focus on the hard things. BUT that same God who is rich in mercy gave me peace and joy. As I look forward to this Christmas, my husband is "cancer-free" but still in a long recovery from cancer and surgery. My job is to choose daily, hourly, minute by minute to turn to the Lord and His grace to carry me through.

Romans 8 | Ephesians 2 | James 1

Romans 8:23-28
"Not only so, but we ourselves, who have the firstfruits of the Spirit, groan inwardly as we wait eagerly for our adoption to sonship, the redemption of our bodies. For in this hope, we were saved. But hope that is seen is no hope at all. Who hopes for what they already have? But if we hope for what we do not yet have, we wait for it patiently.

In the same way, the Spirit helps us in our weakness. We do not know what we ought to pray for, but the Spirit himself intercedes for us through wordless groans. And he who searches our hearts knows the mind of the

Spirit, because the Spirit intercedes for God's people in accordance with the will of God.
And we know that in all things God works for the good of those who love him, who have been called according to his purpose."

James 1:2-5, 12-17
Consider it pure joy, my brothers and sisters, whenever you face trials of many kinds, because you know that the testing of your faith produces perseverance. Let perseverance finish its work so that you may be mature and complete, not lacking anything. If any of you lacks wisdom, you should ask God, who gives generously to all without finding fault, and it will be given to you. But when you ask, you must believe and not doubt, because the one who doubts is like a wave of the sea, blown and tossed by the wind. That person should not expect to receive anything from the Lord. Such a person is double-minded and unstable in all they do.

Blessed is the one who perseveres under trial because, having stood the test, that person will receive the crown of life that the Lord has promised to those who love him.
When tempted, no one should say, "God is tempting me." For God cannot be tempted by evil, nor does he tempt anyone; but each person is tempted when they are dragged away by their own evil desire and enticed. Then, after desire has conceived, it gives birth to sin; and sin, when it is full-grown, gives birth to death.
Don't be deceived, my dear brothers and sisters. Every good and perfect gift is from above, coming down from the Father of the heavenly lights, who does not change like shifting shadows.

Twenty One - My Grandmother

My grandfather had passed away when I was young, and she was left behind. So she lived alone. We visited her often. She would bake the best chocolate chip cookies in the world. We would play in the park across the street from her house. On holidays all the aunts and uncles and cousins would come too. Some summers, I would spend a week or more there with her while my parents were away. She would make the best cookies. Did I say that already? We would eat a simple lunch together and talk about "those men going to the moon" or "the depression" or coal furnaces or the orphanage down the street. Eat and talk. I wish I had listened better, especially about the Depression.

Sometimes in the afternoon, when I would come in from the park, she would be sitting in her chair. She would have dozed off. As I slammed the screen porch door, she would wake up with a start. It was then that I got it. She was alone. She was an old woman living alone. If it weren't for us coming by, for family, she would just doze off. No one would wake her. No one would talk to her.

I am sure you have had a widow in your family. Maybe you are one. Naps and chocolate chip cookies are not the full story. Feeling sorry and stopping by for pity's sake is not the story either. What is? Valuing. Loving. Listening. Learning. Much can be gleaned from those who are older in years. Maybe it is just sitting and having a simple lunch and talking. Laughing. Crying.

Since my grandmother passed away, I have had a habit, whenever I enter a room and see an older person, to go and speak with them. They have much to share. More so, we have much to give back. They were here before us, they made a way, they have suffered on the road, and they have made much of what we have possible. They are to be honored.

So, what about you? If you have a widow in your family, enjoy. If you don't have a widow, can we encourage you, for your benefit, to get to know one? Some widows have few relatives in town, and they would love to get to know you and share stories with you. They are a blessing, and you can be too. You can talk and eat at the same time.

My mother became a widow, my mother-in-law is a widow, and perhaps my wife will be a widow. I know that many who are younger would benefit from spending time with her after I am gone. She now makes the best chocolate chip cookies in the world.

So, can I encourage you today to look around? Family, friends, and even in the mirror and ask what God would have you do?

Psalm 146:9 | Philippians 2:1-3 | 1 Timothy 5:5

Psalm 146:9
The Lord watches over strangers; He supports the fatherless and the widow, But He thwarts the way of the wicked.

Philippians 2:1-3
So if there is any encouragement in Christ, any comfort from love, any participation in the Spirit, any affection and sympathy, complete my joy by being of the same mind, having the same love, being in full accord and of one mind. Do nothing from selfish ambition or conceit, but in humility count others more significant than yourselves.

_____
_____
_____
_____
_____
_____
_____
_____
_____
_____
_____
_____
_____
_____
_____
_____

Twenty Two – Love

Sometimes it is just good to be reminded. Jesus loves you. He really does. If you have received Him as the one who saves, the one who has paid your debt, the one who is king, and the one who is coming again, He loves you. In fact, He loved you before you loved Him. This piece could end there. That is all that needs to be said.

But, I want to say a few more things because for most of us, it is hard to know, experience, and feel the love of Jesus. In part, it is hard to feel the love of Jesus because we are broken, and we live in a broken world. The reception simply is not always so good. But, there are some things that we can do to help us understand better that He loves us.

We can be honest when we aren't feeling His love. Hiding your discontent with an apparent lack of God's affection does not help, so we suggest you share it. Not in a "poison spreading" sort of way, but in a way that expresses your disappointment. Saying it, may release the pressure that is building. You don't need to play the victim, but it you do not have to pretend that everything is all right. You will need to find someone safe to do that with.

We can surround ourselves with things that have been known to help; great music, reading helpful books, and being with godly encouraging people. Those three things have helped others know that Jesus loves them, and there is no reason to think they won't help us. It is important to choose carefully so you might get some suggestions from people you spiritually respect.

We can go to the Bible and combine it with prayer. Note I said combine. When you don't feel loved, reading the Bible can be a bit flat. So, pray and say, "I want to hear from You God and know You are real". If you get in the Word and ask God to meet you, He will open your eyes to the truth. We're not suggesting you just open the Bible, pick a passage, and hope for divine inspiration. We do recommend you take time to immerse yourself in the Word and see what the Story of Jesus is really all about, from Genesis to

Revelation.

Lastly, we could ask ourselves the hard question, "Do I love Him?" Sometimes, if a relationship has gone cold, it is my fault. What do you do if that is the case? You do the same things. Be honest, surround yourself and go to the Word. You might also throw a little repentance in there somewhere. Along the way, the flame will be lit because the reality is He does love you.

That is where we started, isn't it?

Psalm 119:9-16 | John 15:8-18 | 1 John 4:18-20

Psalm 119:9-16
How can a young person stay on the path of purity? By living according to your word.
I seek you with all my heart; do not let me stray from your commands.
I have hidden your word in my heart that I might not sin against you.
Praise be to you, Lord; teach me your decrees.
With my lips I recount all the laws that come from your mouth.
I rejoice in following your statutes as one rejoices in great riches.
I meditate on your precepts and consider your ways.
I delight in your decrees; I will not neglect your word.

_____
_____
_____
_____
_____
_____
_____
_____
_____
_____
_____
_____
_____
_____
_____
_____
_____

Twenty Three - The Toy You Had to Have

One year my sister wanted "the toy of the year"; she wanted a Go-Go My Walking Pup. In the tradition of Cabbage Patch Kids and Tickle Me Elmo, demand far outstripped the supply of the toys. My parents searched high and low for one to no avail. Then on Christmas Eve, a friend called to say that she had found an extra one. One catch, she was in the next state over. So, my parents dropped us off at a friend's house on Christmas Eve and drove to get the toy my sister had to have.

They were so excited to be able to give her the toy she really wanted and looked forward to watching her open it the next day. On Christmas morning, she tore off the wrapping and screamed with joy and surprise that the toy she wanted was hers. Everyone was so happy, and it was a great Christmas.

You know what I'm going to tell you next, right? Yep, a few weeks after Christmas, that toy had been relegated to the forgotten toys pile. It turns out that the commercial made it seem much easier to use and maneuver. Basically, the dog went forwards and back and sometimes struggled to do that. So we played with it some, but it didn't live up to everything she'd hoped it would be.

Does it seem as though our lives are like this a lot? We hope and pray and strive for something, and when we get it, we are so happy, and then it isn't everything we'd hoped it would be and we are disappointed. As adults, things are not typically as simple as I want a toy, and God gives it to me. Prayers don't get answered like that, at least not typically. Instead, often what I think I want gets changed as the Lord changes my heart. That thing that I thought I couldn't live without now holds no interest to me, or maybe it does, but I have a whole new perspective on it.

Through prayer and the power of the Holy Spirit, the Lord can change my heart to desire what He wants for me. It is a daily, hourly, minute-by-minute process to keep our hope focused in the right place. It's okay to desire things, to want things to work out, but where is our hope found? Is our hope in things here on earth, or is our hope in the Giver of all good gifts?

Psalm 119 | Romans 8:24-27 | 1 Thessalonians 2:18-20

Psalm 119:33-37
Teach me, O Lord, the way of your statutes;
*   and I will keep it to the end.*
Give me understanding, that I may keep your law
*   and observe it with my whole heart.*
Lead me in the path of your commandments,
*   for I delight in it.*
Incline my heart to your testimonies,
*   and not to selfish gain!*
Turn my eyes from looking at worthless things;
*   and give me life in your ways.*

Romans 8:24-27
For in this hope we were saved. But hope that is seen is no hope at all. Who hopes for what they already have? But if we hope for what we do not yet have, we wait for it patiently.
* In the same way, the Spirit helps us in our weakness. We do not know what we ought to pray for, but the Spirit himself intercedes for us through wordless groans. And he who searches our hearts knows the mind of the Spirit, because the Spirit intercedes for God's people in accordance with the will of God.*

_____
_____
_____
_____
_____
_____
_____
_____
_____
_____
_____
_____
_____
_____
_____

Twenty Four - Are You Singing Off Key?

Our church staff gets together once a week to pray for requests that come during the week. We get together on Tuesdays and spend about 45 minutes praying for these requests (among other things). In preparation to pray, we often sing a bit and listen to the Word.

Just before Christmas, I happened to be standing next to someone in staff prayer. Let's call her "Jackie" just to protect her identity. Anyway, as we were singing, I felt like my voice, and hers were not in synch. It sounded odd and scratchy. I thought, "Is she singing off-key a bit?" I kept on going, as did she. I kept hearing this slightly off-key voice, though. I thought it must be her, but I knew she was a good singer. But, it seemed to be her. I was conflicted. I had seen her up front leading the congregation in worship. So, I thought she must have a decent voice, but yet it sounded so "off".

There was only one way to make sure, so I did it. I stopped singing. Oddly, the poorly pitched voice went away. It was me. I was out of synch with her. Now I had a decision to make. Do I just not sing? Or, do I continue singing, knowing that I was the one with the problem? I sang. I tried to get my voice a little more in sync with hers. And you know what? She never said anything to me. She may not even remember the event. My guess is that she often has poorly pitched people standing next to her.

Here is the reality for me; I am the one off-key. If I will silence myself, I can listen to Him and hear that He is speaking beautiful and clear truth. Not one note is off-key, just perfect pitch. So if you are hearing something that seems to be dissonant, check your heart first. Then, can I encourage you to listen to His voice? Maybe even try to get in synch with what you are hearing Him say. Don't worry about perfect pitch because the good news is that He won't belittle you - or laugh at your attempt. Why? Because, "The LORD your God is with you, he is mighty to save. He will take great delight in you, he will quiet you with his love, he will rejoice over you with singing" (Zephaniah 3:17).

Ezekiel 11:19-20 | Luke 6:44-46 | 2 Thessalonians 2:13-17

2 Thessalonians 2:13-17

But we ought always to give thanks to God for you, brothers beloved by the Lord, because God chose you as the firstfruits to be saved, through sanctification by the Spirit and belief in the truth. To this he called you through our gospel, so that you may obtain the glory of our Lord Jesus Christ. So then, brothers, stand firm and hold to the traditions that you were taught by us, either by our spoken word or by our letter.
Now may our Lord Jesus Christ himself, and God our Father, who loved us and gave us eternal comfort and good hope through grace, comfort your hearts and establish them in every good work and word.

Twenty Five - All It Needs Is A Little Love

It's the classic scene at the end of "A Charlie Brown Christmas" where Linus says, "I never thought it was such a bad little tree. It's not bad at all really; maybe it just needs a little love". Then all the Peanuts characters scramble their arms around and magically turn the sad little tree into a beautifully decorated tree. Charlie Brown then comes out and sees what all his friends have done for him. I love this scene, but in truth, I love the whole special. It's a young boy searching for the true meaning of Christmas, beyond the presents and commercialism. His friends give him many possible theories: presents, money, community involvement, but Charlie Brown isn't buying it. Then Linus tells him the true meaning of Christmas out of Luke 2. I read that there was a lot of push back to having Linus recite Luke 2. But Peanuts creator, Charles Schultz, was adamant, saying, "If we don't tell the true meaning of Christmas, who will?"

The same is true for all of us. If we will not share with others the true meaning of Christmas, of Christ's love for us and the gift of eternal life, then who will?

This year, I want to keep my heart focused on the love of the Father and give it away to those around me - to look around for ways to share God's love. There are so many ways we can do this. Bring cookies to someone who is lonely; help out with winter chores for elderly neighbors, shoeboxes, or angel tree gifts for the needy. There are more ways to share the love of Jesus than time, so pick some and do them. You will be as blessed as those you are serving.

All they need is a little love. How will you give it away this year?

2 Corinthians 8:7-9 | Titus 3:4-5 | 1 John 4:7-10

2 Corinthians 8:7-9
But just as you excel in everything, in faith, speaking, knowledge, and in all earnestness and in the love we inspired in you, see that you also excel in

this gracious work. I am not saying this as a command, but as proving, through the earnestness of others, the sincerity of your love as well. For you know the grace of our Lord Jesus Christ, that though He was rich, yet for your sake He became poor, so that you through His poverty might become rich.

Titus 3:4-5
But when the kindness of God our Savior and His love for mankind appeared, He saved us, not on the basis of deeds which we did in righteousness, but in accordance with His mercy, by the washing of regeneration and renewing by the Holy Spirit,

1 John 4:7
Dear friends, let us love one another, for love comes from God. Everyone who loves has been born of God and knows God. Whoever does not love does not know God, because God is love. This is how God showed his love among us: He sent his one and only Son into the world that we might live through him. This is love: not that we loved God, but that he loved us and sent his Son as an atoning sacrifice for our sins.

Twenty Six – Home

Dorothy in the Wizard of Oz said it: "There is no place like home!" Better still, Perry Como, The Carpenters and others sing of it this time of year, "...for the holidays you can't beat home, sweet home!"

Home means different things to different people. For some, the sweet aroma of cookies baking and the crackling of a fire bring back memories of beautiful evenings with friends and family. For others, home conjures up less appealing images: a family argument, too much to drink for Uncle Ned, and overcooked ham. In either case, we all know that deep down inside, we want and need home. We want to feel safe and be loved. We want to be cared for and have someone around who will listen to us. We want to be nurtured and we want to feel that we are part of a family.

At this time of year, many people do an amazing job of decorating their homes. You may visit some of them. The decorations are meant to mark the season and enhance the warmth of the home. Perhaps you decorate your house and then go look at others.

Now I wonder, as you walk around other people's homes, if you are bit jealous? After all, "That tree is gorgeous. Those angel figurines are divine and the table setting is to die for!" Hmm. Did we just kill the spirit of this whole thing? On the contrary, we say, let your desires outstrip your pocketbook. What? Yes, as you visit homes this season and see the beautiful decorations, I want to ask you to look at the beauty and feel the fact that it is costly.

It is fine to long for something that you cannot purchase. Why? Because, that thought may take you to the heart of the season: Something was purchased that you could not afford; something grander than angel figurines and the finest china. Jesus came to purchase you. You are the decoration. You are the gift. All that is needed is a home to put you in.

He has even taken care of that. He has prepared an eternal home for those who look to Him; a place where it is safe and all will feel love and care. That home is what you are longing for: to be close to Him, to feel His love, and to celebrate being in His family.

So if you have roamed this year, now may be the time to enter back in. C.S. Lewis once said, "If I find in myself desires that the world cannot meet, it must mean I was made for another world." That is exactly what we believe. We were made for another world, and mysteriously, that world has in part collided with our world by a baby being born in, not a home, but a stable.

Matthew 7:10-12 | 1 Corinthians 6:19-20 | 2 Corinthians 9:14-15

1 Corinthians 6:19-20
Do you not know that your bodies are temples of the Holy Spirit, who is in you, whom you have received from God? You are not your own; you were bought at a price. Therefore honor God with your bodies.

2 Corinthians 9:14-15
And in their prayers for you their hearts will go out to you, because of the surpassing grace God has given you. Thanks be to God for his indescribable gift!

_____
_____
_____
_____
_____
_____
_____
_____
_____
_____
_____
_____
_____
_____
_____
_____
_____
_____
_____
_____

Twenty Seven – Let Us Find Our Rest In Him

This hymn is sung in most churches over the holiday season.

"Come thou long expected Jesus, born to set thy people free
From our fears and sins release us; let us find our rest in Thee." –
Charles Wesley

There is so much to unpack in just two short lines. Are we really longing for Jesus to come again, or if He showed up, would we say, "Oh Jesus, thanks for coming, but I am super busy this week and actually next week, too. Maybe you could come back in a month or so?" Okay, that's a ridiculous exaggeration, and hopefully, none of us would say that to Jesus' face, but are we essentially doing that through our lives each day? We busily run from task to task and, some days, never even think of Him. The good news: God loves us anyway. Even more good news: it is never too late to find our rest in Christ. He holds the power to release us from sin and to wipe away every fear. All we have to do is rest in Him.

If that sounds easier said than done, that's because it isn't easy, and it isn't a one-time thing. As humans, we are prone to wander and forget that our hope and rest is in Christ. That's why regular time in the Word and in communion with God is so important.

We often become so consumed and focused on the world around us that we miss the bigger picture. This can especially be true during the holidays. In Luke 2:25, the scriptures talk about a man named Simeon, "It had been revealed to him by the Holy Spirit that he would not die before he had seen the Lord's Messiah". So he waited, anxiously anticipating His arrival, and when the spirit moved him, he went to the temple and saw the Lord, and his response was profound: "Sovereign Lord, as you have promised, you may now dismiss your servant in peace" (Luke 2:29). He didn't ask for more time or anything else. His soul was at peace, and life was complete.

Mark 13:33 reminds us, "Be on guard! Be alert! You do not know when that time will come." Let's remember today that this world is fleeting. For today at least, let's fix our eyes on the world to come and live our lives preparing for the day when He returns.

Psalm 33:21-22 | Luke 2:25-35 | 2 Timothy 4:7-9

Psalm 33:21-22
For our heart is glad in him, because we trust in his holy name.
Let your steadfast love, O Lord, be upon us, even as we hope in you.

Luke 2:25-35
Now there was a man in Jerusalem, whose name was Simeon, and this man was righteous and devout, waiting for the consolation of Israel, and the Holy Spirit was upon him. And it had been revealed to him by the Holy Spirit that he would not see death before he had seen the Lord's Christ. And he came in the Spirit into the temple, and when the parents brought in the child Jesus, to do for him according to the custom of the Law, he took him up in his arms and blessed God and said,
"Lord, now you are letting your servant depart in peace,
  according to your word;
  for my eyes have seen your salvation
  that you have prepared in the presence of all peoples,
  a light for revelation to the Gentiles,
and for glory to your people Israel."

And his father and his mother marveled at what was said about him. And Simeon blessed them and said to Mary his mother, "Behold, this child is appointed for the fall and rising of many in Israel, and for a sign that is opposed (and a sword will pierce through your own soul also), so that thoughts from many hearts may be revealed."

_____
_____
_____
_____
_____
_____
_____
_____
_____
_____

Twenty Eight - Holiday Giving

We all want the holidays to be a time of joy, family, laughter, giving, and receiving - as they should be! We should go to someone's house for dinner, we should celebrate, and we should cherish the time we have with loved ones. A point should be made to give gifts and to give a little something to those who have less.

For some, this may be the hardest holiday season ever. Jobs may be scarce, and anxiety about money is high. You may be nervous about spending money or may, in fact, not have any to spend. Times might be tight. Now, you might think that I could encourage you and say things like, "O well, we have each other and our health. Those are the important things!" or "What is important is being together, not the gifts you get or give." Those would be true and good words, but I am not going to say them.

Frank Houghton, during the darkest of days on the mission field in China, wrote this,

Thou who wast rich beyond all measure,
All for love's sake becamest poor
Thrones for a manger didst surrender,
Sapphire-paved courts for stable floor.
Thou who wast rich beyond all splendour,
All for love's sake becomes poor.

Thou who art God beyond all praising,
All for love's sake becamest man;
Stooping so low, but sinners raising
Heavenwards by thine eternal plan.
Thou who art God beyond all praising,
All for love's sake becamest man.

When we remember that He became poor, then we can enter into our poverty and see that we are called by "the poor one" to give freely of whatever we do have: our time, a cup of tea, a hug, a bowl of soup or a smile to others in His name and for His kingdom's sake. When we do that, and when we are grateful for Him, in His state of poverty, we do not waste our hard economic time.

So can I encourage you not to waste the "less" that you have? Look to Him and see that He is all we need. Have a warm and wonderful holiday.

Proverbs 22:2 | 2 Corinthians 8:9 | 2 Corinthians 9:8-10

Proverbs 22:2
The rich and the poor meet together;
*   the Lord is the Maker of them all.*

2 Corinthians 8:9
For you know the grace of our Lord Jesus Christ, that though he was rich, yet for your sake he became poor, so that you by his poverty might become rich.

2 Corinthians 9:8-10
And God is able to make all grace abound to you, so that having all sufficiency in all things at all times, you may abound in every good work. As it is written,
"He has distributed freely, he has given to the poor; his righteousness endures forever."
He who supplies seed to the sower and bread for food will supply and multiply your seed for sowing and increase the harvest of your righteousness.

_____
_____
_____
_____
_____
_____
_____
_____
_____
_____
_____
_____
_____
_____

Twenty Nine – Christmas Lights

One of my favorite Christmas traditions every year with my husband is to pick up Christmas coffees or hot chocolate and drive around the city looking at Christmas lights. We listen to Christmas music and discuss the ones that we like the best and why. We really like the spiral Christmas tree displays that have been showing up a lot recently and think that the giant inflatables are generally overused (although we have a friend who uses them, and his display is incredible), but that's just us.

This past year, we noticed that there were a bunch of houses that did not have any Christmas lights out. I said to my husband, "Where is their Christmas Spirit? Can you believe they don't have any lights?" Then we drove up to our own home and realized that we were like most of those homes. Other than candles in the windows, we had no lights on the outside of our house either. So if we weren't doing it, how could we be judging others for doing the same thing? Oops. So after Christmas, I bought décor for our lawn, and this Christmas, we will be ready.

But all of this got me thinking, do I do this in other areas of my life? Do I hold others to an ideal standard that I am not even trying to meet?

The truth is that God's standard finds us all lacking. The standard is perfection (Matthew 5:48), and none of us are perfect, as much as we hate to admit it. But that's why He sent his Son, to save us, to pay the debt that we could never pay, to make us blameless in His sight. He loved us so much that He came to earth to save us, and the cost to save us was so high that no one else could do it, and we could never pay it on our own. That's the true meaning of Christmas: that Christ came to save us because we cannot save ourselves.

In the midst of the lights, decorations, gifts, and parties - let's remember to give thanks to our Lord for the amazing gift of His love and salvation.

Psalm 62:1-2 | John 3:1-21 | Romans 6:23 | Hebrews 5:7-10

Psalms 62:1-2

For God alone my soul waits in silence;
from him comes my salvation.
He alone is my rock and my salvation,
my fortress; I shall not be greatly shaken

John 3:16-21

"For God so loved the world, that he gave his only Son, that whoever believes in him should not perish but have eternal life. For God did not send his Son into the world to condemn the world, but in order that the world might be saved through him. Whoever believes in him is not condemned, but whoever does not believe is condemned already, because he has not believed in the name of the only Son of God. And this is the judgment: the light has come into the world, and people loved the darkness rather than the light because their works were evil. For everyone who does wicked things hates the light and does not come to the light, lest his works should be exposed. But whoever does what is true comes to the light, so that it may be clearly seen that his works have been carried out in God."

Romans 3:23

for all have sinned and fall short of the glory of God

Romans 6:23

For the wages of sin is death, but the free gift of God is eternal life in Christ Jesus our Lord.

_____
_____
_____
_____
_____
_____
_____
_____
_____
_____
_____
_____

Thirty- Underneath

As we approach Christmas, we thought it could be a good time to reflect on what is underneath. It is so easy for us to get caught up in all the events and activities of Christmas: trees and decorations; presents and food; trying to decide if you should switch to low-fat eggnog. Not that there is anything intrinsically wrong with those things, but we want to be sure we remind you to focus on what is underneath.

It is Jesus.

He is the One who is center stage and the One to whom we must give our affection. Anything less would be unhealthy for us, and a dishonor to Him. So we want to invite you to take a short time out. It could be as little as ten minutes. We would love for you to open a bible and read the story of Christmas by yourself. It may be very familiar to you or maybe you have never read it in its entirety. It does not matter. Can we encourage you to read it again? Just get to a quiet space and take time to let it soak in. It is rich.

We believe the Word of God is living and active and that includes the Christmas narrative. We believe it can re-instill hope in your heart and help you to see reality. We think if you will take time to be with Him this week, He will bless you and remind you that He came for you. He will gently whisper that He calls you to come to the manger, come to the cross and then go to those He loves for His namesake and bless them in His name. It could be a moment to cherish. It could change the rest of the week for you.

Some of you will be alone for Christmas. Others will be with people who are hard to deal with. Many will celebrate well with friends and family. Whatever your context is, we want to encourage you to put Christ in the center. He is the one who is the light of the world and your heart. He came for you.

Soon it will all be over. The tree will come down and the lights will be turned off; but not this week. This week is a week for you to reflect on the incarnation of Jesus, the Word made flesh; the One who dwelt among us.

Luke Chapters 1 and 2

Luke 2:8-20

And there were shepherds living out in the fields nearby, keeping watch over their flocks at night. An angel of the Lord appeared to them, and the glory of the Lord shone around them, and they were terrified. But the angel said to them, "Do not be afraid. I bring you good news that will cause great joy for all the people. Today in the town of David a Savior has been born to you; he is the Messiah, the Lord. This will be a sign to you: You will find a baby wrapped in cloths and lying in a manger."
Suddenly, a great company of the heavenly host appeared with the angel, praising God and saying,
"Glory to God in the highest heaven, and on earth peace to those on whom his favor rests."
When the angels had left them and gone into heaven, the shepherds said to one another, "Let's go to Bethlehem and see this thing that has happened, which the Lord has told us about."
So they hurried off and found Mary and Joseph, and the baby, who was lying in the manger. When they had seen him, they spread the word concerning what had been told them about this child, and all who heard it were amazed at what the shepherds said to them. But Mary treasured up all these things and pondered them in her heart. The shepherds returned, glorifying and praising God for all the things they had heard and seen, which were just as they had been told.

_____
_____
_____
_____
_____
_____
_____
_____
_____
_____
_____
_____
_____
_____

Thirty One - Silent Night

Lo in the silent night A child to God is born.
And all is bought again That here was lost, forlorn

Could but thy soul o man Become a silent night?
God would then be born in thee And set all things aright
-source unknown, modernized by R. Schlichting

The original source of this quote is somewhat obscure, but in any case, I modernized it for us. I would love for you to read it aloud slowly, trying to get the rhyme when you are in a place that you feel comfortable in doing so.

It may first remind you of the hymn, Silent Night. But look again. Imagine the night He was born. A purchase began on that night to buy what had been lost. The word forlorn means forsaken and nearly hopeless; that is what it was like before the Son came to make all things right. People were desperate. And then He came as a child, grew to be a man and lived perfectly. He died a beautiful death that we might be set free.

Read the second stanza again, if you will. Just as the night became silent to receive the once and future king, could your heart again become silent? There is a lot of noise during the holiday season, and the author is calling for us to be still in the midst of it. He may be speaking to those who have never received Him as Savior, God would then be born in the, and he may be talking to those who need a re-birth of sorts, a re-kindling of the gospel in their hearts. In either case, when He comes, He sets all things right.

That is what we need this season. To have all things be set right. That does not mean that all of our troubled relationships will be restored or our circumstances will change. It means that in our souls, we will rest in the fact that He is good and He loves us. We can be silent and receive what He has for us in light of that.

So, can your soul become a silent night for sixty seconds? We pray it can.

Deuteronomy 27:9| Micah 7:7 | Romans 5:1-5

Deuteronomy 27:9
Then Moses and the Levitical priests said to all Israel, "Keep silence and hear, O Israel: this day you have become the people of the Lord your God.

Micah 7:7
But as for me, I will look to the Lord; I will wait for the God of my salvation; my God will hear me.

Romans 5:1-5
Therefore, since we have been justified by faith, we have peace with God through our Lord Jesus Christ. Through him we have also obtained access by faith into this grace in which we stand, and we rejoice in hope of the glory of God. Not only that, but we rejoice in our sufferings, knowing that suffering produces endurance, and endurance produces character, and character produces hope, and hope does not put us to shame, because God's love has been poured into our hearts through the Holy Spirit who has been given to us.

_____
_____
_____
_____
_____
_____
_____
_____
_____
_____
_____
_____
_____
_____
_____
_____
_____
_____
_____

Thirty Two - Broken Glass

I had a roommate once who loved to work with stained glass. Nothing big like what you would see at St. Paul's Cathedral, but he did small pieces for friends and family. One day, he showed me how it was done. Each piece of glass was carefully chosen and then cut to match the next piece. Next, he wrapped a foil around the rough edge of the cut piece and heated it up with a small blowtorch as he deftly applied some solder to the mix. The two became one. He then went on to the next piece.

Initially, I could not tell what was being formed or what the picture was. But, over time it became apparent. When it was done, it was a beautiful red rose surrounded by a white background. When we held it up to the light, it became both dazzling and peaceful at the same time. It was a beautiful work completed.

Maybe you are reading today, and your life is shattered. Perhaps things have happened to you that should not have, or you have done things you regret. As you sit here, you may be thinking that your future is black and dark because your past has been. You might see yourself as a shard of glass that has no use, no future, and no hope. You are just broken.

Well, you are right on one count. You are a shard of glass. We are all broken pieces of glass: jagged, rough, and in need of a loving hand to pick us up, cut us to size, and wrap some foil paper around our edges. If you are thinking you have no use, future, or hope, we want to encourage you to look to the One who puts together the grand mosaic we call the Kingdom.

He will make the rough places smooth as you submit to His loving care. He will wrap you up and give you a place of great importance. He may put a little heat on the situation, but it is always designed for His good purposes. He knows, as well as you may secretly know, that the picture cannot be complete without you in it. When He does complete the work, He will hold us all up to the One for whom we have been made, and it will be both dazzling and peaceful.

So you are not worthless, in whatever place or situation you find yourself today. We invite you to give yourself up to the Craftsman, God the Father, and come join the community of His people. One note of caution; we too are broken glass, sinners, in need of His hand. Sometimes we even scrape against one another, and it hurts a bit. Sometimes it cuts, but we know we are all part of the mosaic, finer than anything adorning the windows of St. Paul's Cathedral.

So we continue to build and love one another, knowing that one day we will all shine like the sun before Him. As you come across stained glass this holiday season and beyond, remember your part in the mosaic and let His light shine through you.

John 1:1-18 | 1 Corinthians 1: 1-9 | 1 John 1

John 1:1-18
In the beginning was the Word, and the Word was with God, and the Word was God. He was in the beginning with God. All things were made through him, and without him was not any thing made that was made. In him was life, and the life was the light of men. The light shines in the darkness, and the darkness has not overcome it.

There was a man sent from God, whose name was John. He came as a witness, to bear witness about the light, that all might believe through him. He was not the light, but came to bear witness about the light. The true light, which gives light to everyone, was coming into the world. He was in the world, and the world was made through him, yet the world did not know him. He came to his own, and his own people did not receive him. But to all who did receive him, who believed in his name, he gave the right to become children of God, who were born, not of blood nor of the will of the flesh nor of the will of man, but of God.

And the Word became flesh and dwelt among us, and we have seen his glory, glory as of the only Son from the Father, full of grace and truth. (John bore witness about him, and cried out, "This was he of whom I said, 'He who comes after me ranks before me, because he was before me.'") For from his fullness we have all received, grace upon grace.

For the law was given through Moses; grace and truth came through Jesus Christ. No one has ever seen God; the only God, who is at the Father's side, he has made him known.

1 John 1
That which was from the beginning, which we have heard, which we have seen with our eyes, which we looked upon and have touched with our hands, concerning the word of life— the life was made manifest, and we have seen it, and testify to it and proclaim to you the eternal life, which was with the Father and was made manifest to us— that which we have seen and heard we proclaim also to you, so that you too may have fellowship with us; and indeed our fellowship is with the Father and with his Son Jesus Christ. And we are writing these things so that our joy may be complete.

This is the message we have heard from him and proclaim to you, that God is light, and in him is no darkness at all. If we say we have fellowship with him while we walk in darkness, we lie and do not practice the truth. But if we walk in the light, as he is in the light, we have fellowship with one another, and the blood of Jesus his Son cleanses us from all sin. If we say we have no sin, we deceive ourselves, and the truth is not in us. If we confess our sins, he is faithful and just to forgive us our sins and to cleanse us from all unrighteousness. If we say we have not sinned, we make him a liar, and his word is not in us.

Thirty Three - Will He Come?

Christmas Eve is special in our house. I am so looking forward to the night! Our whole neighborhood sets out luminaries (bags with sand and candles for the uninitiated). On the drive back from church, I see candles that have been lit by other neighbors glowing along the side of the road. It warms my heart and causes it to race at the same time. When I pull into our driveway, I quickly walk into the house, and I smell it: Christmas Eve dinner, prime rib. Dorothy cooks it to perfection, and I cannot even describe to you all the trimmings. It is amazing. And then there is dessert! I hear the Christmas music playing amidst the laughter of daughters and mothers. I know my part, so I enlist a daughter and light our luminaries and then a fire in the fireplace. Dinner is served!

After dinner, we will walk down the street to our friend's house, and he will read "The Night Before Christmas" to my kids. He has done that for 14 years in a row. It will be a great evening. Even as I write, I wish it were here. We will be together, and there will be great joy.

The word Advent is from the Latin ad, which means "to" and vent, which means "come." That is pretty simple: To come. That is what we look for during this season; the coming. We do celebrate the birth of Christ and reflect on His ministry on earth as well as His death and resurrection. But more so, we should look towards the future. We want Him to come to reclaim and redeem all things finally and fully.

I wonder if that helps you or if it takes the wind out of the Christmas Season? For me, it is a bit convicting. I do get wrapped up in parties, decorations, food, gifts, and family reunions during this time of year so much that I forget to look forward. In fact, I can be pretty content with the "now" and not think so much about what is to come.

Just as we prepare for Christmas Eve this year, we should prepare for the second coming of Christ. How do we do that? Well, Paul, in his letter to the Thessalonians, helps us. He says, "Since we belong to the day, let us be self-controlled, putting on faith and love as a breastplate and the hope of salvation as a helmet." We are called to prepare as a bride prepares for a wedding, as a mother cooks for Christmas dinner, as a father and daughters light luminaries. We are called to live as citizens of the city to come when He descends in all His glory and brings with Him the new heaven and new earth. We will all be together, and there will be great joy. He will come, and what a feast it will be when he does!

Psalm 38:21-22 | Psalm 62: 5-6 | Mark 1: 14-20

Psalm 38:21-22
Do not forsake me, O Lord!
 O my God, be not far from me!
Make haste to help me,
 O Lord, my salvation!

Psalm 62:5-6
For God alone, O my soul, wait in silence,
 for my hope is from him.
He only is my rock and my salvation,
 my fortress; I shall not be shaken.

_____

_____

_____

_____

_____

_____

_____

_____

_____

_____

_____

_____

_____

_____

_____

_____

_____

Thirty Four – A Gift for the One Who Has Everything

So how much do you have left to buy? Maybe a better question is, "How much do you have left to spend?" In a few days, you will be giving and receiving. We all know that the giving and receiving of gifts at Christmas time is a reflection of the great gift we have received in Christ. It is good to give gifts of time and treasure to those around. We especially want to remember those who are less fortunate.

Do you know what your loved ones want and/or need? Men are hard to buy for, especially dads. My kids ask me every year. I know I may be one of the more challenging people for whom to buy a gift. Socks, some underwear, and maybe a new belt are my kind of gifts. This year, I really would like a DVD set of my favorite TV show and a significant gift certificate to the smoothie shop in town, but that is about it.

So what about Him? Have you thought about what you might bring Him this Christmas? After all, it is His birthday. I am not advocating gold, frankincense, or myrrh. The latter is very hard to find these days in any case. So what will you give Him?

I wonder if we can challenge you all this year. Give Him, Jesus, a gift. What do you get for the God who became man and has everything? Do you need ideas? Well, first of all, think about what His love language might be. Could it be time spent, acts of service, or words of affirmation? It is something to think about. Perhaps Jesus' list might include these: "Love my people a bit more (act of service); listen to me by reading the Bible, talk to me from time to time (time spent), or put some of your idols down and see me more as the King (words of affirmation)." You get the idea.

Now here is the challenge: write it out and put it in an envelope with His name on it.

"Jesus, for your gift this year, in special celebration of Your birth on earth, I want to give you: _____. I know I will fail, and I will need the Spirit to empower me; but I give this to you as a gift, as an offering!"

First thing Christmas morning, open His presents. Read the cards to one another. It is His birthday. Then, share amongst yourselves and enjoy.

Romans 11:28-36 | 2 Corinthians 9:6-15

Romans 11:28-36
As regards the gospel, they are enemies for your sake. But as regards election, they are beloved for the sake of their forefathers. For the gifts and the calling of God are irrevocable. For just as you were at one time disobedient to God but now have received mercy because of their disobedience, so they too have now been disobedient in order that by the mercy shown to you they also may now receive mercy. For God has consigned all to disobedience, that he may have mercy on all.
Oh, the depth of the riches and wisdom and knowledge of God! How unsearchable are his judgments and how inscrutable his ways!

"For who has known the mind of the Lord,
   or who has been his counselor?"
"Or who has given a gift to him
    that he might be repaid?"
For from him and through him and to him are all things. To him be glory forever. Amen.

2 Corinthians 9:7
Each one must give as he has decided in his heart, not reluctantly or under compulsion, for God loves a cheerful giver.

_____
_____
_____
_____
_____
_____
_____
_____
_____
_____

Thirty Five – Rights

You have them. The right to remain silent. The right to bear arms. The right to free speech. The right to own property. You have rights in this country. People have actually fought and died so that you can have rights. That is freedom. We in America celebrate freedom. It was hard-won. Independence from tyrannical rule is a wonderful thing.

Now here is the twist, and it comes in two forms. The first is a question. Are you living under tyrannical rule? We don't mean in the political sense. We mean in the spiritual sense. Are you living under the direction of your sin nature that says, "Do this!" and "Do that!" Are you responding to that which is dark and that which really wants to keep you in bondage? It could be in the shape of a bottle, or a credit card, or a naked woman on a screen. It may come to you in the shape of a shopping mall or a weight scale. Perhaps it is a sneaky idol like jealousy or discontent with your lot. Whatever it is, we say, "Down with tyranny!" This is a day we call you to live as free men and women because Christ has set you free.

The second form of twist is this: you do not have to use your rights. Even in the examples above, you could talk, not own a gun, or not talk. By definition, a right means that you may or may not do it. You don't have to. You can lay down your rights. Here we enter into the fuller mystery of the gospel. Jesus had all power and all rights. He did not live under tyranny, giving in to the dark side. He was perfectly and joyfully obedient. We call that the active righteousness of Christ. Then He laid down His right to life that He might overcome the tyrannical rule of another. He accomplished it. We call that His passive righteousness.

So because the great freedom fighter came to set us free on both counts, we are able, by His power, to resist the temptation to live in bondage, and we can enjoy the full freedom that comes in laying down our rights joyfully for the sake of others. That is freedom!

John 10:10-12| 1 Corinthians 9:1-15 | 1 John 3:11-24

John 10:10-12

The thief comes only to steal and kill and destroy. I came that they may have life and have it abundantly. I am the good shepherd. The good shepherd lays down his life for the sheep. He who is a hired hand and not a shepherd, who does not own the sheep, sees the wolf coming and leaves the sheep and flees, and the wolf snatches them and scatters them.

1 Corinthians 9:1-3

Am I not free? Am I not an apostle? Have I not seen Jesus our Lord? Are not you my workmanship in the Lord? If to others I am not an apostle, at least I am to you, for you are the seal of my apostleship in the Lord. This is my defense to those who would examine me.

Thirty Six - There Is Still Time

The countdown to Christmas seems like it started in October. Now, it is nearly here. However, there is still time. You might be asking, "Time for what?" Well, you have time to go back to the store. For some of you, that thought is crazy. For some of you, that is certain. There may really be a few more things to pick up, even if just from the grocery store. Get some cranberries or sweet potatoes. Maybe you still have not purchased that one gift for that special someone. So, go if you must, or if you want. The stores will close on Christmas Eve. The countdown is almost done.

We would love for you to continue, or begin, another countdown as the shopping season ends. Begin a countdown to Christ. This one does not have days or hours attached to it because it is a countdown that continues. We wait with our candles lit, with our voices lifted, and with our hearts hopeful. We wait for Him to come - or us to go. We wait, knowing there is still some time but not knowing how much.

In the Dickens classic, "A Christmas Carol," Ebenezer Scrooge is shown the past, present, and future in a new light. While it is not a gospel narrative in many ways, Dickens points to something central to the gospel at this time of year. Seeing his sin, Scrooge begs for a chance to change, a chance to be different. The "ghostliest" of the spirits takes him to a dark place, but he does not leave him there. In a dramatic scene, Scrooge says, "Your nature intercedes for me and pities me. Assure me that I may yet change these shadows you have shown me by an altered life!" He is on his face, and the petition is granted. Did Scrooge just "will to change?" Maybe he did, but it seems the spirits somehow enabled him.

If there was a sequel, perhaps we would see him reverting to his old miserly ways. We would enter the story here. Some of you have had an encounter with the Spirit. Change has happened, yet you know that the nature of Scrooge is still with you. Petition again; He intercedes for you. Some of you are just now seeing what the Spirit is showing you. We are glad and say, "Keep coming!" Some of you may be wondering, "Is there a Spirit?" For everyone, we hope that the verses today will be helpful as you think about your past, present, and future. There is time, time to go to a store where we can buy gold refined in the fire. This purchase will enable us to make things right with the One we have offended, to ask forgiveness for not loving well, and to say, "I love you." There is still time, but we do not know how much.

The baby born on Christmas Eve, the second person in the Trinity, is the One who brought change. The third person, the "ghostly" Spirit, is the One who presses it into the hearts of Scrooges like us. It is good to admit we are misers: misers in our natural man and misers who are the recipients of the grandest gift. So, the countdown to Christ continues. A milepost on the way will be the candlelight services held all over the world on Christmas Eve.

Isaiah 55 | Mark 13:32-35

Isaiah 55:12
For you shall go out in joy and be led forth in peace;
the mountains and the hills before you shall break forth into singing, and
all the trees of the field shall clap their hands.

Mark 13:32-25
But concerning that day or that hour, no one knows, not even the angels in heaven, nor the Son, but only the Father. Be on guard, keep awake. For you do not know when the time will come. It is like a man going on a journey, when he leaves home and puts his servants in charge, each with his work, and commands the doorkeeper to stay awake. Therefore stay awake—for you do not know when the master of the house will come, in the evening, or at midnight, or when the rooster crows, or in the morning.

_____
_____
_____
_____
_____
_____
_____

Thirty Seven - Inexpressible Joy

I knew he was going to lose it. I was to officiate the wedding of the daughter of a close friend of mine. The night before the wedding, we had the rehearsal in the chapel—what a great setting. The groomsmen and bridesmaids took their places on stage. We recessed out and then practiced coming in to the music. As my friend walked his daughter down the aisle, it hit him. He began to tear up as he approached the front of the chapel. We paused. It was a wonderful moment.

Why did he cry? Well, he told me that they were not tears of sadness. He likes the guy his daughter married. He told me that they were tears of inexpressible joy. He went on to explain that sometimes words cannot express how we feel. Tears can. The thought of his daughter, the bride, marrying the man she loves, the bridegroom, brought him to tears of inexpressible joy.

Now as Christians, there is something deeper that is happening in a marriage ceremony. It is a picture. We see it in the 21st chapter of Revelation, "I saw the Holy City, the new Jerusalem, coming down out of heaven from God, prepared as a bride beautifully dressed for her husband. And I heard a loud voice from the throne saying, 'Look! God's dwelling place is now among the people, and he will dwell with them. They will be his people, and God himself will be with them and be their God.'"

Imagine the Father, seeing the bridegroom (His son Jesus) as the bride (the church) comes forward at the end of time for the consummation of all things. That will be a moment of inexpressible joy, and that may well be why He will wipe every tear away. It will be a joyous occasion.

For now, we are called to look for a glimpse. We may see it in a daughter's wedding. A Christmas Eve service with candles and joyful voices singing praise to God might give us a taste. We might find it as someone we know comes to faith. We may experience it as our souls are healed through confession, repentance, and forgiveness. It is just a glimpse of glory, and there is more to come. He is the God who gives inexpressible joy.

Romans 12: 11-13 | Colossians 1:3-14 | Jude 1:17-25

Romans 12:11-13
Never be lacking in zeal, but keep your spiritual fervor, serving the Lord. Be joyful in hope, patient in affliction, faithful in prayer. Share with the Lord's people who are in need. Practice hospitality.

Colossians 1:3-8
We always thank God, the Father of our Lord Jesus Christ, when we pray for you, since we heard of your faith in Christ Jesus and of the love that you have for all the saints, because of the hope laid up for you in heaven. Of this you have heard before in the word of the truth, the gospel, which has come to you, as indeed in the whole world it is bearing fruit and increasing—as it also does among you, since the day you heard it and understood the grace of God in truth, just as you learned it from Epaphras our beloved fellow servant. He is a faithful minister of Christ on your behalf and has made known to us your love in the Spirit.

Jude 1:24-25
Now unto him that is able to keep you from falling, and to present you faultless before the presence of his glory with exceeding joy,
To the only wise God our Savior, be glory and majesty, dominion and power, both now and ever. Amen.

Thirty Eight - Does It Make Any Difference?

For many, it has been a hard year. Many have suffered. People were born and people have died. In a way, it may feel like a repeat of the last year, the year before, or ten years ago. What difference does a year make as people reflect again on the fact that 2,000 years ago, Jesus came as a baby to a young mother and father? What difference does it make that He grew up as a man, lived a perfect life, and died a brutal death to save His people from their sins? What does it matter that He rose from the grave and ascended into heaven? Maybe it does not matter. Perhaps it does not make a difference that He lived, died, and rose again.

Now, as that paragraph shocks your system, can we say something? It really may not matter. You see, all Jesus is, and all He did does not matter if you have not received the gift of Him. If you have not said something like, "He is the choicest one!" or "I am in need of only what He has to give me!" then it doesn't matter. He is yesterday's news, and the last year, the last ten years, or the next twenty years do not matter. Outside of Christ, nothing matters. Outside of Christ, there is just "Christmas, another year over," as John Lennon wrote. Unless you have repented and turned to Him, it does not matter.

We want it to matter for you. We want you to look back on this year and know that it made a difference because He is the "fact of the matter," and we are one year closer to Him returning in glory. He is why this year mattered. He is the hope to whom we cling.

He is why we can cry out, even as we look back on an "annus horribilus," and say, "Thank you Lord Jesus" and "Come Lord Jesus! Make all things right!"

So as you turn the page on this year, can we ask you to check your heart and see if it matters? We believe He is calling His own to come with him to the next year of the King.

We long for your life, the "anno domine" we just completed, and the year to come to matter. It was, is, and will be a year of the King. Long live the King!

Matthew 28:1-5 | 1 Corinthians 15

1 Corinthians 15:51-58

Behold! I tell you a mystery. We shall not all sleep, but we shall all be changed, in a moment, in the twinkling of an eye, at the last trumpet. For the trumpet will sound, and the dead will be raised imperishable, and we shall be changed. For this perishable body must put on the imperishable, and this mortal body must put on immortality. When the perishable puts on the imperishable, and the mortal puts on immortality, then shall come to pass the saying that is written:

"Death is swallowed up in victory."
"O death, where is your victory?
O death, where is your sting?"

The sting of death is sin, and the power of sin is the law. But thanks be to God, who gives us the victory through our Lord Jesus Christ. Therefore, my beloved brothers, be steadfast, immovable, always abounding in the work of the Lord, knowing that in the Lord your labor is not in vain.

_____
_____
_____
_____
_____
_____
_____
_____
_____
_____
_____
_____
_____
_____
_____
_____
_____

Thirty Nine – Angst

We celebrated forty years of marriage by taking a Greek cruise. During the depths of COVID, cruise lines were deeply, deeply discounted, so yes, it was a deal. We went with two other couples but decided to take a few days before we met them by ourselves in Cyprus. So that was the plan. To get on the ship, we had to be vaccinated. We also had to have a negative COVID test no more than three days before getting on the ship. We had heard of others who had arrived at the ship, were tested, and found to be positive. No cruise for them! Now we were traveling thousands of miles, had paid the fare, and I was anxious. What if? My sin nature said, "Maybe you could fake the test!" but thankfully, I had too much Christ in me for that.

Still, I worried. I thought maybe we could take a test four days before (as we would be in Cyprus for three days), and if that was negative, we could use that. But four days is not three. We would have to take a test in Cyprus at our expense. We would have to wait for results, and worse, if we were positive, we would be stuck in Cyprus. Condemned to Cyprus. We went. When we got off the plane in Cyprus, they ushered us onto a bus, took us to a terminal, and we went through immigration. As we stood in line, I noticed that those completing immigration were being "shepherded outside" to people who were doing COVID tests on the spot. They had decided to randomly test the whole plane! They sat us down, "up the nose," and asked for all our contact information. Then we left for our hotel. Later that night, we got emails saying we were negative. It was such a shock just to be told, "Sit down, we are testing you!" But we were glad it happened. It was over. And we were negative. We had what we needed. Freedom. No condemnation, and we could take the next few days and enjoy.

What are you worrying about in this season? Do you worry about how you will be received? Are you concerned that you will be accepted? Will you be welcomed at the table? Much is out of your control: how the adult children will receive you, how the boss will ultimately make decisions about your job, and how your relatives will act towards you at Christmas dinner. But the Lord who came on Christmas is 100% in control. He has pre-planned. And here is the good news: He has tested you. You are clean, and you are accepted for entrance because He has applied the work of Jesus to your soul. You have a righteous record, his record. You can enter into His presence. You are "not condemned," and that means freedom. You can enjoy the days ahead and rest in Him!

Romans 8

Romans 8: 1-2
Therefore there is now no condemnation at all for those who are in Christ Jesus. For the law of the Spirit of life in Christ Jesus has set you free from the law of sin and of death.

Romans 8: 31-32
What then shall we say to these things? If God is for us, who is against us? He who did not spare His own Son, but delivered Him over for us all, how will He not also with Him freely give us all things?

_____
_____
_____
_____
_____
_____
_____
_____
_____
_____
_____
_____
_____
_____
_____
_____
_____
_____
_____
_____
_____

Forty - No Resolution

Well, do you dare? Do you dare to not make a New Year's resolution? It seems that everyone has at least one: Exercise more! Read more! Or find a new job! There must be something you want to resolve to do in the New Year, and January is a good time for a fresh start, right?

Actually, it probably is not the best time to start. Statistics show that most resolutions are not kept for more than a few weeks. That is the cold truth so, you might not want to bother. That is not "reverse psychology." It is just a fact. Now, instead of making a resolution, perhaps we could think about why we cannot keep resolutions.

How about this as a resolution: "Resolve: To find out why I do not keep resolutions!" Are you interested? God says we should not make a vow, and then break it. He does seem to be interested in us keeping our word. Maybe that is a good place to start.

The Lord does not change; He decrees, and it happens. He wills, and it comes to pass. He has created us in His image and for His pleasure, and He has prepared acts of service that we might walk in them. He has also created us to be dependent on Him. So what are we saying? Jesus is the one who is the covenant keeper. Christ in you is both the hope of glory and the One that you are to live through by faith. Belief is what you need, and He is the one to give it.

Let us try this: "Resolve: To believe!" What do we need to believe? No, who do we need to believe? We need to believe Him. If you "work" to that end this year, you may see other things come together. Ask Him for faith to believe that the word of God is living and active. When you get it, you may find yourself hungry for the study of the Word. Ask Him for the faith that He will supply all your needs according to His riches, and as it grows, you may find yourself less anxious about the future. When you find yourself not believing, repent. Make that your resolution: to believe and repent, and then use the means of grace, the Word, prayer, and the sacraments to help.

Does it sound strange? Maybe it is a bit unorthodox. We might refer back to the Gospel of John. When they asked Jesus in John 6 what they needed in order to do the work God required, He said, "Believe in the one He sent." It can't hurt, can it? Resolve: to believe!

Matthew 8:5-13 | Mark 9 | Acts 10:42-44

Matthew 8:5-13
When he had entered Capernaum, a centurion came forward to him, appealing to him, "Lord, my servant is lying paralyzed at home, suffering terribly." And he said to him, "I will come and heal him." But the centurion replied, "Lord, I am not worthy to have you come under my roof, but only say the word, and my servant will be healed. For I too am a man under authority, with soldiers under me. And I say to one, 'Go,' and he goes, and to another, 'Come,' and he comes, and to my servant, 'Do this,' and he does it." When Jesus heard this, he marveled and said to those who followed him, "Truly, I tell you, with no one in Israel have I found such faith. I tell you, many will come from east and west and recline at table with Abraham, Isaac, and Jacob in the kingdom of heaven, while the sons of the kingdom will be thrown into the outer darkness. In that place there will be weeping and gnashing of teeth." And to the centurion Jesus said, "Go; let it be done for you as you have believed." And the servant was healed at that very moment.

Mark 9:24
Immediately the father of the child cried out and said, "I believe; help my unbelief!"

Acts 10:42-44
*And he commanded us to preach to the people and to testify that he is the one appointed by God to be judge of the living and the dead. To him all the prophets bear witness that everyone who believes in him receives forgiveness of sins through his name."
While Peter was still saying these things, the Holy Spirit fell on all who heard the word.*

Made in the USA
Coppell, TX
13 November 2023

24146822R00050